The Lesson Plan: An Educator's Inspiration

K. L. Herald

Copyright April 2014 K. L. Herald

The Lesson Plan: An Educator's Inspiration

By K. L. Herald

Published by K. Herald Developments L.L.C.

Riverview, FL 33568

©2014, K. L. Herald Inc. All Rights Reserved

No part of this publication may be reproduced or distributed in any form or by any means, or stored in a database or retrieval system, without the prior written permission of the publisher.

This book is available in volume for qualifying organizations. Please contact the publisher to inquire.

For more information about this book or to book the author for motivational speaking, please visit www.klherald.com

Cover and interior design by K. Herald Developments, L.L.C.

www.klherald.com

Herald, K. L. The Lesson Plan: An Educator's Inspiration

Includes bibliographical references.

ISBN-13: 978-0-692220474 (pbk.)

Printed in the United States of America

15 14 13 12 11 10 09   06 07 08 09

Table of Contents

Introduction

Chapter 1	Grammar	22
Chapter 2	Classmates	47
Chapter 3	Preventative Measures	55
Chapter 4	Talking to the S.T.A.A.R.'s	65
Chapter 5	Unconventional Connections	83
Chapter 6	Regularity Notice	99
Chapter 7	Stand up and Standout	114
Chapter 8	Conflict of Interest	126
Chapter 9	Driven by Faith	140
Chapter 10	Strengthen the Focus	152
Chapter 11	Value Source	164
Chapter 12	Self-Motivation	172
Chapter 13	An Educator Inspired	189
Chapter 14	The Toolkit	199
Chapter 15	Transparency	206

ACKNOWLEDGMENTS

"One of the most honest and open stories I've read from a teacher and administrator." R. P. Washington, HIM Tech Medical Professional

"K. L. Herald just has a way with people. Maybe new educators will be able to learn a few of her tricks through her writing." Anonymous

"Using your education in collaboration with your unique personality will not only educate your audience, it will also keep them entertained." K. L.

DEDICATION

To my mother for entertaining my thoughts and encouraging me to dream with the lights on.

Introduction

Some people dream of being a classroom teacher. I never had that dream. As a kid, I loved going to school. In my opinion, some of my childhood teachers were superheroes. But I never once imagined myself being a real teacher. Teaching would be the last job I would ever desire to have, or so I thought. Looking back, I now know why I laugh out loud when someone asks me what I do for a living.

I grew up believing in what my grandmother called blessings. Blessings were described to me as simple staples such as food, clothing, shelter, family, and friends. You know, the little things we take for granted like being alive. As a kid, hearing my grandmother say things like, "What doesn't kill you only makes your stronger" and "count your blessings" seemed to resound as just things wise older people say. It wouldn't be until I reached

The Lesson Plan: An Educator's Inspiration

almost 30 years of age that I began to repeat these sayings myself. Moreover, it wasn't until around the same age my career made me think the act of dying would be more accommodating then attempting to be stronger.

Was the profession to teach really a blessing? As I fell further and further into a slump, I felt the career was more of a nightmare. Looking around at colleagues that were rounding off their 30 year career, I wondered how they managed to last so long.

Being introduced to teaching was totally unexpected. The opportunity to actually be a real teacher at a school with real kids and real books was unbelievable. Teaching was suggested to me by someone that was convinced I could be the perfect role model and leader for today's type of a kid. I was flattered and unemployed so I accepted the invitation into a completely unfamiliar world.

The high and lows of teaching came so fast and sporadically I could hardly keep a straight face. I tried to stay strong, smile and toss every struggle up as opportunity to grow. I was a great pretender.

When I attempted to do my best and commit to my role, it seemed like it always resulted in mistakes and missed deadlines. I wanted to quit. Giving motivational speeches to students who could hear my message but weren't actually listening to me grew exhausting. When sitting in parent conferences and listening to the way some parents spoke to me and my fellow co-workers, I doubted if teachers were still respected as professionals. Co-worker conflicts and misunderstandings made me believe that I was the only person alive that sought to diffuse rather than incite problems. Monday morning walks from the parking lot through the hallways to my office upset me because my cheerfully expressed good morning was not returned from fellow colleagues who were dreading the upcoming week.

As the feelings of defeat attempted to steal my joy and effect my character, I resorted to the most welcoming place that always provided consolation; my beliefs. From the classroom to the curriculum office and into my daily life I began to notice that not everyone had the ability to take the negatives and creative a positive spin on this challenging profession.

Somehow I managed to keep it all together and maintain a demeanor of control and confidence. I made sure that I would stay strong for my co-workers and never give any indication that I was in just as much distress as they were. Seamlessly, I allowed my strength to carry me through each and every struggle. Eventually my strength was so evident that people around me began to wonder how I continued to smile during the conflicts and the pressure to complete never ending tasks. But as you all know, what is perceived is not always reality. Sadly, what people did not know is that I was drowning emotionally as an educator.

    I encouraged myself to remain hopeful about my chosen profession and believed that each day things would eventually get better. Unfortunately, with every trying situation I struggled to keep my faith and optimism in regards to education. When in doubt, I sought confirmation from my students. Looking into the eyes of influential young minds each day strengthened my personal commitment to persevere and endure the struggle of doing what I believed to be the right thing to do. The belief that there is a higher power directing my steps, for reasons out of my control, kept me from asking, "Why is this happening to me?" For some reason I just knew that something good would happen if I continued to just keep it all together and concentrate my energy on helping others. I never thought a profession in education would provide me with a purpose. It did.

    I knew that one day I would be chosen to lead in some capacity. I never imagined that the calling to lead would be in the role as a high school administrator. Even further from my train of thought, was the possibility of education shaping me into an inspirational leader. As I reconfigured stress and tribulation into triumph and promotion, I concluded that being a leader is about withstanding. Somehow, I was blessed to understand how things can be painful and rewarding at once. Embracing both personal and professional change caused me to help others do the same.

Thinking back to all the times I was reprimanded, insulted and exhausted I didn't realize I was growing professionally. Through all the various situations and challenges that I have encountered, I now realize that all along the struggle was preparing me for my purpose. With the assurance of faith and trust that the plan for my life had been predetermined, I stuck with education. The crazy part of it all is that I actually learned to like all the madness and stress that a career in education so graciously provided. I started to embrace the profession of educating, which created a hunger to

The Lesson Plan: An Educator's Inspiration

learn and figure out almost everything around me. An understanding for what was happening in my career consumed me. The struggles as an educator propelled me to become more than a public employee. I learned how to motivate others. Each morning I wanted to share a story that would inspire him or her of many doubts. I not only wanted to teach and motivate the students, teachers and staff at my school, I wanted to say or do something that would shift the mindset of others and empower them with the same energy to motivate and inspire. I know, to some it sounds crazy and reading my last sentence probably made you say to yourself, "Give me a break!" I almost said the same thing when I came up with this idea. But as struggle influenced me to extend my reach, the world around me began to reach back.

Instagram and Twitter followers commented on daily quotes. Former students left testimonies on how conversations with me helped to shape their own career and personal lives. "Why not tell my story to the world?" I thought to myself. With my audience providing feedback in relation to my thoughts, enthusiasm and advice; I must be on to something. So I took the steps to share my story, beliefs, and encouragement with the world around me.

Without a solid plan as to how I would communicate this message into the hearts and minds of others, I began writing what I believed to be everyday experiences as I developed my career in education.

Several thoughts traveled through my mind as to who my target audience would be as I began to

The Lesson Plan: An Educator's Inspiration

write. Oddly, the more I wrote, the more I felt my target audience grow. I wondered if this work would be primarily relevant to educators. Could aspiring educators value my experiences and see purpose in the career path they were planning to take? Should this literary work be used as reference when a current teacher or administrator needs direction in overcoming a potential or present obstacle? There were moments when I slammed the laptop shut and said to myself, "Let's be real, you aren't even a writer." Who was I kidding? Nevertheless, I felt I had something to say. If just one person finds relief from my words and learns from my experiences; that would be the biggest reward I could ever receive. Somewhere, somebody could very well be in need of direction. Regardless if the reader is a student, future teacher, veteran teacher or administrator, my experiences could assist someone in need of inspiration.

So here it is, The Lesson Plan: An Educator's Inspiration. This work is created with the intention of transforming the mindset of any striving professional. The accounts are simultaneously relevant and helpful to both new and experienced professionals. This work illustrates the highs and lows of a rewarding profession with an opportunity for you the reader, to reflect on your own professional experiences. In each chapter, I describe a personal experience that shaped me professionally and motivated me to pursue my dreams. Even though the experiences I will share are primarily in education, I have learned from conversations with non-educators that my story is not uncommon. In general, any professional who is seeking to improve and grow professionally can find value from this transparent resource. I invite anyone to use my experiences to create their own form of motivation and implement The Lesson Plan: An Educator's Inspiration towards accomplishing professional goals.

If this work falls short of its motivational and inspirational goal, maybe the world will at least empathize with educators. The laughter that fills my heart as I look back at my toughest moments reminds me that I have been blessed to make it through those challenge times. It also reinforces my belief that my story should be told. All the tough moments as a classroom teacher and as an assistant principal made me a leader. As I attended meetings with other professionals in the field, I could hear their concerns and desires. I could see their desire to lead. Sharing my story with others just might bring out the leader in someone else.

This book was written with the intention to influence and inspire anyone entering or working in the field of education. Every success I have experienced in my life stems from the world of education. The strength that I have gained was taught to me through my journey as an educator. That unfamiliar world of education eventually not only made me stronger but it enabled me to unknowingly strengthen others. May this book be an inspiration to the reader and serve as a blessing to all.

The Lesson Plan

The Lesson Plan

Chapter 1

Grammar

K. L. Herald

What started out as a routine conversation with my internship mentor, evolved into the moment I was convinced I needed to begin writing and telling my story as an educator. Sitting in that office with my mentor I started to review the steps that led me to my current frustration. As a graduate student, I was well on my way to earning a master's degree in educational leadership. Working a full time job at a new worksite and completing my internship requirement had me questioning my sanity. As part of the internship I was required to perform and record practice experiences as a school administrator.

My mentor, which happened to be a seasoned administrator showed me the ropes and signed off on my paperwork as proof. He was a good guy with a wealth of experience and had a knack for entertaining my sorrows. Flopping down in the chair across from his desk, I pressed the back of my head against a whiteboard mounted behind me. Looking up at the ceiling I shook my head and asked,

"What have I done so badly to end up here?"

He couldn't answer my question; all he could do is laugh.

"You're on that again?" he replied as he fumbled through his usual stack of discipline referrals.

The recent changes in my life, primarily my work site, had my head spinning and my stomach in knots.

Being extremely unhappy was an understatement. Due to a recent transfer in work location, I'd lost myself and needed a reason to continue on as an educator. With a semester remaining in my plight to receive a master's degree in Educational Leadership, I was stressed out from being a full-time teacher and graduate student.

You see, as a graduate student I was well aware of the internship requirement for my master's program. When I made the initial decision to continue my education, I predicted I would be at my old work site. But a recent move and change of address made it difficult to make the 40 minute drive to and from work. The sensible decision was to transfer to a school site closer to home. Without so much as a second thought, I interviewed and accepted the position all in less than a 3 hour time span. Knowing very little about the school I now had transferred to, I would have to finish what I started, my 300 hour internship requirement in order to receive my master's degree in Educational

The Lesson Plan: An Educator's Inspiration

Leadership. Ironically, I ended up completing my internship at a school site that seemed like a foreign country. I honestly felt I'd transfer to a school overseas rather than across town.

In actuality, it was one of the most respected middle schools in the county. My new school site had been recognized to no end for triumphs and successes such as, at the time, obtaining an "A" ten years in a row, based on the state's school grading system. The school's reputation of excellence carried not only through the school but also throughout the surrounding community. Working at this new school was a personal life adjustment. My new boss was a principal that ran the site with a stern authoritative hand. She was the kind of boss that would make you question why you were at the vending machine during your break instead of planning for the next 4 weeks of class. She gave you the feeling that even at your best; you still weren't doing things the right way. I don't think she realized just how much power she had. Then again, maybe she did.

The kids that attended the school were just as odd to me as my new boss. The population of students was total opposite of the students I taught prior to my change in work location. Culture shock was causing hair loss and headaches. I went from bringing in old clothes for my students who were unable to afford clothing to seeing kids wear clothes so expensive, I couldn't even afford them with a full-time job. I wanted to go back to where I'd come from.

Sitting there in the office that afternoon to do my usual administrative practice activity, I was ready to either leave teaching or leave the school. At

The Lesson Plan: An Educator's Inspiration

the onset of my third year of teaching, I was beginning to question my abilities and my drive for the profession. As my mentor and I sat and discussed my many frustrations, I began to reflect on my current experience and tried to find a gold lining somewhere in my discontent. I was far from what some would describe as a veteran in the world of middle school teaching. In my opinion I still had a lot of learning to do. Up until my third year of teaching, I was eager to perfect my craft and own my title as teacher. But as of recently, I began to hate the decision that I made 3 years ago to become a teacher. More so, I was regretful of my decision to transfer to a school that stripped me of all my sense of belonging and importance. I just wanted to go back to the school where I'd started; a school I like to refer to as RMS.

RMS was located in an area that looked and felt like the neighborhood I grew up in. The school was surrounded by older homes. The cars that were parked along the street and in the driveways were just as old as the homes. On my first visit to the school I reminisced about my middle school experience. The older building wasn't great, but it was enough. The teachers weren't the most polished, but they loved their job and the kids they taught. The kids, they had their issues. But just as those kids accepted the old building and the realities within it, they accepted me. They didn't just view me as a teacher; they viewed me as an extension to their world.

RMS was described as a Title I school. Now some you are probably wondering what a Title I school is. Title I is the description used if your student body is comprised of a large number students that depend on the school for breakfast and lunch. This usually means that your surrounding community is made up of families that are considered to be of low-socioeconomic standing. To keep it simple, average hardworking families with a parent or parents doing the best they can to make ends meet. Working at a Title I school I found that families were less involved but trusted me as the professional. Often, parent phone calls were not returned and when they were, I was told that it was my responsibility as the teacher to change the student's behavior or make sure the student was turning in homework assignments. Thus, a Title I school site had given me my first skill set as a teacher.

In two years of teaching at RMS, I never felt uncomfortable or inadequate. I was never questioned by parents about my education or teaching experience. My co-workers were down to earth and were always ready to talk and share stories. My principal at RMS even treated me like I was a part of his school family and welcomed me knowing I'd never done the job. Things were good at RMS and I now regretted ever leaving there.

Unlike RMS, my new school site was located in an affluent area just outside the city. Most students at the site were from affluent families and were very receptive to the opportunities education could bring. The 1,520 student population consisted of 1,073 white students; a grouping that totaled 70.59% of the school's population. When I was introduced to the demographic of the site and agreed to take the position, I had no idea that the schools culture would be completely opposite from where I'd come from. Much less, I never thought this new school site would be such a learning experience.

Problems that I faced did not stem from my lack of experience in teaching. The source of my problems was that I had not been in an environment where both parents and students were so concentrated on the importance of school and education. The expectation of the students and parents was nothing like I'd experienced at RMS. The students in my classroom challenged me as a professional. The parents of my students did the same. At this new school, I was a teacher being pushed to a new level. My teaching was part of the stepping stone in preparation for high school and beyond. I felt like I was no longer allowed to connect and care for kids, my job was only to teach. The change in my work location was eye-opening to say the least. Having experienced this transition, I had gained a full understanding of the word *demographic*.

Your site demographic can foreshadow what your level of parent involvement will be as well as, student failures and achievement. Each and every day as a classroom teacher is determined by the demographic make-up of your student population. The needs of students in Title I schools many times are different from the needs of students in affluent communities. The overall level of student performance is sometimes lower at Title I sites compared to schools in more affluent communities. Students who have lower scores in reading and math need additional resources like math, writing or science coaches. While students who are excelling in core courses may need additional tutoring for advance placement courses.

    My role changed when I transferred from RMS to my new school site. I went from acting as a school mom, counselor, sponsor, disciplinarian and coach to just an educator. Realizing that I had grown accustomed to my initial role in education, acclimation to my new surroundings was nothing short of a struggle. My former students were comparable to me and shared similarities like being a product of a single-family home and adjusting to changes that stem from living on a low income. I became comfortable being an educator that shared commonalities with my students and the parents of my students.

Had I been in affluent areas before? Yes. Had I taught brilliant students in my short career? Absolutely. The reality was that my vision of teaching was created by kids in an area I was comfortable with. I had never been out of my own element. I was lacking certain experiences that would fully shape me as a well-rounded educator. Being a teacher in a Title I school setting was all I knew how to do and I was comfortable in that capacity. Unknowingly, routines or habits that I picked up in the onset of my career would create an awkward situation and momentarily cause me to question my ability to do the job. To my surprise, I would learn that being comfortable is not always the best mindset to have or position to be in.

The moment I was made aware of my own shortcomings surfaced during a scheduled observation that was conducted by my principal, who I referred to as the warden. The observation was specifically for teachers with less than 3 years of service within the county. For teachers, observations are usually done by a principal or assistant principal. A rubric or evaluation tool is used to measure your effectiveness and overall job performance. For most teachers, being observed is the most stressful part of the job. Some school districts use observations to determine your pay or whether or not you keep your job the following year. With the pressure on, I knew I had to put on my best performance.

During my observation, I threw myself into my usual show and captured my young audience. By no means was I as awesome as I described myself to be, but in my mind I was a good teacher. I circulated the room, posed questioned to my students and checked for engagement and understanding. I was teaching. The warden never displayed a facial expression to indicate her thoughts or feelings, so I wasn't seeking gratification from her mannerisms. It wasn't until the post observation conference that I was privy to her thoughts and an opportunity to receive her feedback.

As she opened the observation conference she began with a question.

"What school did you teach at prior to coming here?"

I responded to her question with a puzzled look on my face.

"Oh, ok, well…I just have a few areas of improvement for you to consider."

The Lesson Plan: An Educator's Inspiration

At this point I knew I would be looking online for a new job in the morning based on what she was about to say. Needless to say I was super afraid of the lady and I had already been warned she wasn't one for compliments. Ironically, the conversation didn't pan out the way I thought it would. The one criticism about my teaching ability was concentrated on my grammar.

"Excuse me?" I stated and I moved closer to the desk of the principal sitting across from me. I focused on the sound of her voice. My attention was focused on her every word.

"Be mindful of the use of double negatives when instructing your class," she said to me as she attempted to smile. I shook my head and accepted her feedback. "Proper grammar is important. The kids can pick up those improper habits and we don't want that to happen."

I respectfully responded to her statement with a nod and asked if there were any other areas I needed to improve on. Making reference to my possible return to a Title I site if the opportunity presented itself, I was now convinced it was time for me to go. I already felt unsuccessful in the job and her words seemed to support that reality.

She looked at me and said, "Be patient, there may be some changes soon with new possibilities for you right here."

Without responding and neglecting to think about her last statement, I walked out of the office and immediately began to reflect on my previous two years of teaching. I concentrated on her comment about my speaking and the fact that no one had ever criticized my grammar.

On prior observations I received above average ratings and feedback from my former principal. In comparison to other new teachers, I was adjusting to the position well. Tons of compliments and praise would come from my parents in the form of emails and cards. All the prior feedback I received led me to believe that I was an effective teacher and a role model for students. After the post conference that pointed out my improper grammar, I then questioned what factors are important to educating a child.

Let's back track for a moment, her remarks never stated I was a bad teacher. But in my mind her remarks angered me. I felt offended and inadequate. I received a college degree just like every other teacher on staff. Therefore, I considered myself to be a validated professional. Communication was a personal strength, or so I thought. I attempted to reassure myself, but still had doubts. I wondered if my students thought less of me as a teacher when I made statements that were not grammatically correct.

I knew the language that the average kid spoke. Growing up with a background similar to my students, I was the average kid. I understood their circumstances and struggles. There were times when I quoted song lyrics to popular tracks to redirect and grab the attention of my class. The language most familiar to their world helped me to connect with my students. That broken grammar was a part of my daily language. As I reflected, the only thing that came to mind was the smile on my student's faces when I spoke to them. Moreover, despite the differences between me and my new student population, I was connecting with my students. They loved me for who I was and enjoyed me as a classroom teacher. As I thought back I could hear the sound of laughter from one of my students that seemed to find humor in my remarks. I almost begin to doubt myself even more and my decision to teach when I stopped and said to myself, "This lady is crazy! I'm built for this job!"

The more I thought about the observation remarks the more I wanted to improve as a professional. Being prepared for the worst, I immediately took the principal's feedback from the observation as an insult instead of viewing her words as an opportunity for me to improve as a teacher. After calming down, I accepted her statements as a lesson learned and perceived the feedback as a blessing. She had just given me the motivation to correct my mistakes, improve as a teacher and work towards one day becoming the principal of my own school. That observation was the first set of tools I received for my professional toolkit. It also encouraged me to create my lesson plan; the plan I used to achieve my goals.

The Lesson Plan: An Educator's Inspiration
You are Not Alone

Whether you are training for a position or have been doing a job for 10 years, find someone to talk to when times are hard. Sometimes, the pairing of new and old ideas creates a solution that will positively impact your clientele.

I continually stress to my co-workers that there is no need to reinvent strategies that are already proven to work. Seek to grow from the knowledge that can be provided from others around you.

Research Who, What and Where

When applying for a position or transferring to a new location, find out about the group of people you will potentially work with. Become familiar with the student population. This knowledge will help prepare you for the transition and will prevent the feeling of isolation. Once you are there, seek to connect and learn even more about the people you are working with and the clientele you are seeking to impact.

The Comfort Zone Limitation

Comfort, convenience and familiarity will not lead to personal or professional growth. If you decide to place yourself in a position to experience uncommon situations, you will inevitably learn something new. Routine conversations and predictable occurrences will not expand your knowledge base. Both well rounded leaders and professionals have a broad base of experiences that allows them to extend their possibility to effectively produce positive change.

Take the Step of Separating Yourself from Your Comfort Zone

With the experienced gained from teaching in two different spectrums, both affluent and low socioeconomic communities, I was able to diversify my teaching experiences and strategies. The transition between the two work sites broadened my perception and expanded my level of cultural knowledge. Being able to communicate with both affluent and low socioeconomic families was a valuable skill that is necessary as a teacher and as a school leader.

Be Receptive to Feedback

Not every statement or comment from a superior or co-worker is an insult. Analyzing feedback is an effective way of identifying areas of personal and professional improvement. Think about the feedback given and identify any objectives or practice that can be improved in your position or role. Always look at comments or advice as a growth or learning opportunity. Remember, your goal is to provide your students with the best instructional experience possible.

Administrators will also use feedback as a means to grow and learn. The implementation of feedback will allow your staff to see that you are continually looking for areas to improve; in effect, displaying that you are a concerned leader.

The Golden Rule

During my first years as a teacher, I learned that the key to being an effective teacher is not always about how well you know the curriculum and manage a classroom. Teaching from my heart and treating others the way I wanted to be treated made each transition in my career easier.

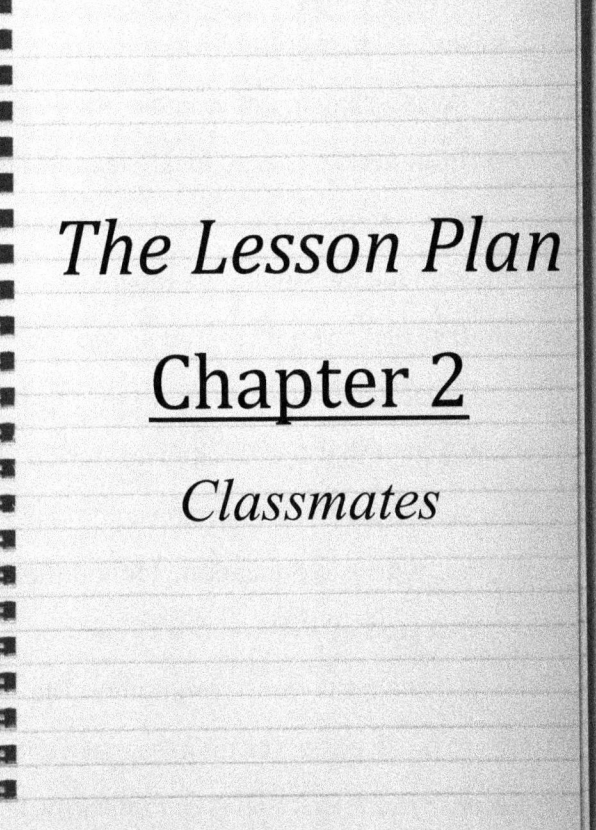

The Lesson Plan

Chapter 2

Classmates

The Lesson Plan: An Educator's Inspiration

By the end of my first year at the new affluent school site I learned to understand my co-workers. Finding co-workers at the school site that were similar to me and my background was not easy. Nevertheless I was willing to get to know others. As time went on, it became easier to locate leaders and colleagues that understood the various minds and hearts of those young individuals we taught. The students whether rich or poor created an inclusive illustration of what public education was made of. I made the connection that the faculty and staffed mirrored the students and surrounding community. I now know this is typical in education. I found that the teachers that worked in this more affluent or well-off school lived in the same community. The connection was much easier for them to make with students because there was a level of familiarity. It dawned on me that this was not intentional, it was just reality.

My perception of my new colleagues were that they were people who didn't joke much, preferred not to socialize outside of school and never uttered profanity during adult conversation, this made them strange to me. So as I sought to meet someone I like to describe as laid back and low-key, I was looking for someone that I could associate myself with. Someone that understood how it felt to be in unfamiliar territory. Someone who was trying create a plan for his or her life with little help or support. Someone who understood differences among people and welcomed the opportunity to embrace something new. More importantly, I was searching for someone that could sympathize with once being a kid that didn't have much except a heart full of dreams, in need of someone to help make them all come true.

There were times when I felt my co-workers had forgotten where they had come from. Then I questioned if any of them came from a single family home or were raised by a single mom that prided herself on doing the best she could. Just like a new student at a new school, I needed to feel as if I belonged. I needed a group of teachers I felt I could connect to. I needed to know that the people I worked with were educating kids because they understood kids. I wondered if my new group of counterparts actually loved kids or if they were just doing their job. I wasn't even sure I was working with the kind of people that lived by the golden rule; treat others as you wish to be treated. Surprisingly, everyone in education does not live by this creed.

There were some on staff that had literally given up on kids completely. As I tried to connect to others at the school that shared my feelings, I felt even more out of place.

My immediate allies became individuals on staff that assumed the role as custodians, secretaries and resources officers. Looking back, at almost every school I've worked at, my crew always seemed to include the support staff. I could easily be found hanging out with the custodians trying to speak broken Spanish or getting the scoop on who was disgruntled or being promoted. Knowing the latest gossip on the job was interesting, but knowing gossip was not a way to increase my knowledge as an educator.

The custodial workers, secretaries, and cafeteria ladies were real people to me that

The Lesson Plan: An Educator's Inspiration

understood life the way I did. But at the end of the day I was a teacher. I loved my crew, but I needed to collaborate and connect with other teachers to grow to the professional level I desired. Unfortunately, without professional dialog and collaboration I was limited in regards to professional growth. I needed to surround myself with a person or people that could challenge my knowledge base as an educator and encourage me to grow in the field of education. My heart was filled with the will to do my best as a teacher.

Then one day it happened. Change would provide new leadership and a breath of fresh air. I was introduced to someone that played a significant role in my career in education, someone that would force me to create and pursue a level of achievement beyond my imagination.

The Lesson Plan: An Educator's Inspiration
Welcome New Faces

Just like a new student on the first day at a new school, new teachers and other staff want to feel welcomed and cared for. It is important that your worksite has a group or committee for helping new employees to become familiar with the atmosphere and culture. Welcoming gestures also provide a sense of care for the new staff member as a person and not just another teacher on staff.

As a staff member, think back to your first day on the job and the things you needed help with. For example, information like the location of employee restrooms and lounging areas are at the top of most people's need-to-know list when starting a new job. New administrators want to be welcomed and trusted too. Leaders want to know that their staff feels optimistic about their capabilities of leading the group. When leadership changes at a site, it's important that the leadership team welcomes the new person. Giving small items such as school spirit paraphernalia is a great way to welcome new leadership staff.

If You are New

Try to find someone just as new as you are. This way you are connected to someone that understands your needs and wants as a new employee. Don't be afraid to ask questions when you have a need or want. Remember, at some point in everyone's career they were new to the job too.

K. L. Herald

The Lesson Plan

Chapter 3

Preventative Measures

The Lesson Plan: An Educator's Inspiration

My career drastically changed direction as I moved to a position that was expectantly offered to me. The warden's prediction was right. There would be changes and new possibilities for me right at this new school site. One day out of the blue, I met a young lady that was convinced I would be a great addition to her leadership team in the role as someone who would motivate and monitor at risk students or potential drop-outs. This young lady had recently been appointed to the position of principal, replacing the warden and her authoritative hand. I would no longer feel as if I was in a correctional facility. With a background in high school teaching and administration, this new leader's perspective and view was more aligned to what I imagined from a lifelong educator. It wasn't until our meeting that I understood a more appropriate word to describe my view and mindset was the word *progressive*.

K. L. Herald

The day she walked into my class I will never forget. I had my students arranged in groups and was circulating the room answering questions when in walks a professional dressed woman that seemed to be finding her way around a new place. As she walked in the room I began to walk in her direction. Every teacher at the school was awaiting the arrival of the new principal and at that moment I just happened to be meeting that individual.

We shook hands in the traditional fashion, exchanged a few pleasantries and made a connection through a few common acquaintances. I explained my teaching assignment and how long I had been on staff. She stepped back and looked at me as if she was confused about something I just said. Moments into our first introduction I felt comfortable enough to say to her, "What? Why are you looking at me like that?"

She immediately replied, "You like teaching History?" with a raised eyebrow.

We looked each other square in the eye and began to laugh. She said that she would rather use me in the role of drop-out prevention and already had certain group of students in mind. I shook my head in acknowledgment and feeling of relief came over me. I wasn't sure what the role of dropout prevention required, but I wanted to think it was an opportunity for me to return to a group of students I could relate and connect to.

Momentarily she was summoned by her tour guide and we agreed to finish the conversation later. As she walked away, a feeling of relief came over me so quickly I wanted to take the rest of the day off. Prior to the leadership change I was stressed to the point of hair loss and anxiety. Being stifled was an understatement. I would no longer feel as if I was working in isolation, fearing my personality would offend a co-worker or cause a parent to complain. I would now be under the leadership of someone who had an infectious personality, genuine interest in kids and an understanding of diversity.

Now at this point you are probably thinking the same thing I was as I stood in front of my newly appointed principal. Did middle school students actually drop out of school? Honestly, my first thought was I would probably be more successful back at a Title I school. Missing being appreciated and not wanting to be corrected for grammatical mistakes gave me reason to consider retracting my steps. But as luck would have it, I was given a reprieve. The opportunity for me to embrace the inner troubled child that I somehow managed to polish up enough with a dress shirt and a college degree had presented itself. Someone saw something in me that I would have never seen in myself.

Even though I had now received my master's degree in educational leadership, I was not yet prepared to work in any type of leadership role. I had less than 3 years teaching experience in a subject area I barely understood. How was I going to convince a student to continue on the educational path? More importantly, how in the world would I ever convince a student that didn't fit the majority demographic that their school was a place of acceptance? It would now be my job to convince students that a chance of academic success was for each and every student; even if you were 15 years old in the 7th grade. I would no longer feel like a prisoner in an uncomfortable place. More so, the unsuccessful student would no longer feel uncomfortable either. Quickly, I found that this group of low performing students was feeling just as uncomfortable as I was.

To be considered a leader, an educational motivator, was a title I never expected to have. Now I'd been asked to step out of the classroom and into what I found to be my most enjoyable position as an educator. I was now able to hone in on a different set of skills that I unknowingly picked up somewhere between birth and the last conversation with my new principal. It was now my responsibility to be a role model and motivate reluctant students. I immediately wondered who was going to spearhead motivating me because there was no way I was about to pull off this new gig. The role required a lot of creativity and time. Without a formal job description and list of required duties, the key would be my personality. To my surprise, I would become something more meaningful to a child's life. I became a source of recognition and one of the reasons that troubled students even came to school in the morning.

See, the students who now were my daily concentration, looked to me to evoke something special within them. Okay, let's keep it real, they just looked to me to recognize if they missed a day or hadn't been in the assistant principal's office for fighting or screaming profanity at a teacher that week. But I was proud of my new role. To me, my troubled population of over aged, underachieving students had given me a purpose.

The Lesson Plan: An Educator's Inspiration
Opportunities Will Find You

One of the concerns that many employees have is that their strength or natural skill set will not be identified and put to good use. The advice that I would give an educator or any professional is to trust your leadership staff. Stressing out over not being selected as a member of a committee or worrying if you will ever be promoted is not conducive to positive output.

Focus your energy on conveying your values, work ethic, and passion for your current position. By making an impact that propels the organization towards achievement and change, you will be valued for your contribution. In many organizations key individuals are viewed as a source of knowledge and are often sought out by others. These key employees are rarely stored in positions that hide their capabilities. Strong contributors are not overlooked, especially if members of the leadership team have a keen eye for talent.

The Lesson Plan

Chapter 4

Reaching for the S.T.A.A.R's

The Lesson Plan: An Educator's Inspiration

Opportunity not only knocked, it kicked the whole damn door down. I became a leader in a capacity that I never expected so soon in my career. The charge to motivate and encourage disconnected students had now taken over my life. I needed a way to make this group of students feel recognized and that they mattered, despite their shortcomings and differences. Being someone that severely lacked creativity, I lost sleep thinking of a name for my new group of students. How would others around school know that these students were working towards a change? I needed a title for the group that would shed light on the positive characteristics of each student and get others to encourage them as well. I wanted to glamorize them individually and cause conversation to help teachers connect to each student personally. A connection to the school and their teachers would lead to increased self-esteem and a new level of acceptance that was not currently in place.

One night before meeting with my new principal about the upcoming role I would assume, I had an "ah-ha" moment and it came to me. My students would be called STAAR's- Student's Targeting Academic and Attendance Rewards. I would use the acronym of STAAR to promote and recognize my at-risk students. Each student had an individual photo posted in my office that included a brief description about themselves below. Students shared blurbs about their favorite holiday or best school related experience. Some students even included their favorite musician or favorite thing to do outside of school. I thought back to my years as a kid wanting to be recognized by the teachers and administrators at my school. So I established processes I felt would be cool for a kid in need of positive attention.

Anytime a STAAR student did well on a test or an assignment I would post their work on a bulletin board that was exclusively for them. If I could get teachers and administrators to take an interest in my at-risk students, I could get my students to see that they were an important part of our school. Somehow I needed to convince them that their performance mattered. I would walk students to the administrative office and have them inform their assistant principal or guidance counselor of their accomplishments. Anything that made the student feel like a STAAR was my plan of attack.

Being responsible for the at-risk population was as if someone rewound the cassette tape back to my childhood. Not knowing exactly what the role of drop-out prevention was supposed to look like, I resorted to my personal experience as a middle school kid. I ran my thoughts by my new principal and she supported my unconventional ideas. My new principal reminded me that it was ok to be myself and allow my past to help guide others.

    I will never forget the day I saw her sit down next to one of my STAAR students and give her undivided attention as the student explained a family situation she was going through. She listened and provided a perspective that had me convinced was a lie. How could this professional, put-together school leader have experienced similarities in her childhood that one of my students could relate to? She was a successful professional that seemed to have life completely figured out. As she reached to hug my student, kiss her on the cheek and boldly state,

The Lesson Plan: An Educator's Inspiration

"You tell them to kiss your butt!" I realized the three of us had much more in common than just being females.

Each of us had endured struggle at some point in our life that made us appreciate others and we had obtained some sort of strength that could compel the most defeated individual. With a smile, snotty nose and a few tears my STAAR student smiled and said "Yes ma'am," and proceeded to class. I was instantly inspired. At that very moment I realized the way to connect to a student is to build a professional relationship which allows students to see you as a real human being. No one is perfect and imperfections remind us that we can still grow and improve. From that moment on I began to share the stories in which my students could relate to. I then identified exactly what my target audience needed; the truth.

When a student has been lied to, the last thing they need is to be lied to by the last glimpse of hope; the teacher. I told my students as I met with them individually in my small office in the back of the guidance suite, that in order to be a STAAR we must shine together. I explained that there are times in life when our parents are working two jobs and can't make it to conference night and we need a Plan B. And if that meant Plan B was granny coming to your school to meet with teachers or your neighbor that always comes over on Friday to drink beer with your dad, it was ok. Having somebody to support you is better than having no one in your corner.

I remember a student by the name of Adam. He was a 7th grade student with a negative attitude

The Lesson Plan: An Educator's Inspiration

and displayed feelings of resentment. This young man always seemed to be angry and looking for any opportunity to express his anger. Upon what was our initial meeting, I recognized Adam's instantaneous need for attention, primarily from a female. He was regularly seen with a girlfriend engaging in what seemed to be misunderstanding about the plan for the weekend, or a phone call not returned. It seemed his method of communication was to argue. I remember how he became a STAAR student as clear as if he was sitting next to me telling his story today.

Adam found a connection through a teacher at the site that lived in his neighborhood. This teacher didn't know Adam's family but had drawn a conclusion based on Adam's stories of arguments with his grandma and him being on restriction for longs periods of time. This teacher and neighbor approached me and said, "I think this young man needs someone like you." I agreed to add him to my list and placed him on my roster for progress monitoring thinking there was an academic concern. Adam got to me before I could send a student request to formally meet him and explain the STAAR program. I recall the way he fumed when he spoke of his little brother that lived in another state with mom and how he wondered why she loved the little brother more than him. As he became a member of the STAAR program Adam and I accrued several conversations about what life would be like if he could go and live with his mom.

There were times when I shared his excitement as he anticipated a scheduled phone call from mom over the upcoming weekend. As we walked to the bus ramp I would remind Adam to tell

The Lesson Plan: An Educator's Inspiration

me all about the phone call on Monday. Sadly, Monday mornings never went as Adam or I planned. After several Monday mornings of walking into the guidance office and being greeted by Adam's head down, slumped over in the student waiting area, I eventually felt his pain.

After practically picking him up and walking him to my office, avoiding the looks and inquires of other students as to what's wrong with Adam? I got to hear the excuses. He would explain that mom was planning on calling, but texted instead and said that she didn't have minutes available on her phone to talk to him. He went on to say that sometimes when she called she only talked to Dad long enough to argue about which parent would claim him on the income tax that year. As I listened I couldn't help to think that this was way too much information for a kid to know. I would put the pieces together just enough to carry him through the day and hope that his disappointing weekend would not affect his academic progress that week. Adam remained a STAAR student for the duration of the school year.

    Adam ended the year on a high note and an expectation that his mother would be sending a plane ticket so that he could visit over the summer. Sadly, returning to school after a major summer disappointment of traveling to nowhere, Adam felt empty. He had nothing left to give. He now needed what I avoided giving him all along, the truth. I knew at that point this student didn't need me to lie for his mom's shortcomings. Adam needed honesty. He needed someone to be encouraging and be the one person that explained the difference between reality and what you see on TV.

The Lesson Plan: An Educator's Inspiration

I said to Adam, "There comes a point where you no longer live for others. You create your own plan and you become the person that YOU depend on." I explained to him that he was lucky to have a grandmother that is still alive, more importantly one that is providing food, shelter and love to him. I also stressed the importance of building with the blocks that you already have in your possession. Adam never mentioned his mother again. Neither did I. We moved forward together and he improved his communication, not just with me but other women as well; including grandma.

My experience with Adam contributed another tool to my set of skills. It was with Adam that I realized students' respected honesty. Students want to hear what is real. They do not want to be told fictitious stories that they cannot and will not relate to. Students want to know how you've handled a similar situation and what the outcome was. As we grow up and encounter unfamiliar situations we use our past experiences and hopes to direct our actions. When given honest direction and facts, we increase our chance of being successful. As educators, we are responsible for marketing success and demonstrating that success is possible through hard work, commitment, and honesty. Moreover, being honest with yourself is a major component of personal success.

My time spent with students like Adam also gave me a plethora of knowledge that not only aided me in directing students, but adults as well. It wasn't until the next level in my career that I realized the correlation between motivating students and teachers. During conversations with teachers on campus concerning issues with my STAAR students, I began to realize that broken students grew up to be broken adults. The same soothing words that I spoke to my students were effective in conversations with teachers who were exhausted or just flat-out tired of being disrespected; by students and other faculty members. The progression from student motivator to adult motivator caused me take what I had learned from helping kids and apply it to adults.

The Lesson Plan: An Educator's Inspiration
Working with the Public
When working with the public, especially in public education, you have to be both flexible and understanding. We are expected to provide assistance to others. Reviewing each case-by-case situation individually is key. What worked for one student or family may not work for the next. Take the time to analyze each situation and make adjustments based on individual needs.

Take Time to Listen
We will not be able to fix every problem that walks into our classroom or offices. We can listen and make time to take an interest in others.

As a teacher, knowing your students culture, background and immediate family structure provides an opportunity for you to be forewarned of potential problems and concerns with students.

As a co-worker, providing an opportunity for others to express concern will allow your colleagues and staff to know you have a genuine interest in their needs. Also, you never know when you will need that favor returned.

As an administrator, your staff is comprised of adults that have personal problems and concerns. Some of their problems will arise without warning. Some problems may require that a member of your staff take time off or moments away from the classroom. Some problems may be the result of the administrator's response to the staff member's plea for help. Whatever the case may be, a level of understanding and support for your staff not only as teachers, but as people is required.

Share Your Story
Allow your past to surface and help others. Share your story and don't be afraid to open up to the people around you; students, staff and leaders on site. Sharing a story from your past is part of your Professional Toolkit that is original and personalized. No one has lived your life. This tool can only be used by you.

Just as teachers listen to their students, administrators must listen to the needs of their staff. A leadership staff that models making connections with staff will inadvertently have a staff that connects with the students, parents and stakeholders in the community.

People are People
Both children and adults have personal experiences and emotional baggage in tow. We build from our

past and use the experience to move forward in our lives. We all are the product of our upbringing and environment. Every person at your work site no matter their age, nationality, or origin has a past. Always remember that. Use compassion to build relationships with students, teachers and the community.

Honesty
As a teacher or administrator, we are viewed by the public and trusted to demonstrate appropriate character traits. If we want to continue to receive such recognition as educators, we have to be honest with our students, parents, co-workers and most importantly ourselves. An honest individual will always be respected. Honesty will also allow you to be trusted as a professional.

Own Your Past
Without our past, we would not be able to improve and grow both personally and professionally. Individuality is a gift. No one can provide what you

have to offer because there is only one version of you.

A Leader...
will be transparent to help others. The ability to humble yourself and share past experiences lets others know that you also have encountered difficult times. Use your past struggles as a tool to assist, problem solve and plan.

K. L. Herald

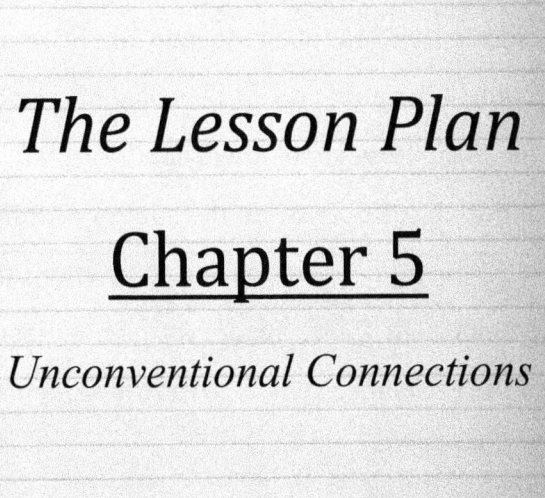

The Lesson Plan

Chapter 5

Unconventional Connections

The Lesson Plan: An Educator's Inspiration

After working with kids for a few years, I could easily identify a child in need of some love and connection. Helping students establish a connection to school became the easiest way for me to create a level of motivation and maintain that momentum.

Coincidentally, my ability to help kids in need of connection and motivation also enabled me to do the same for teachers and others adults on staff. The realization surfaced when the adults on staff were inquiring more about making connections than the students were. It was apparent that the teachers needed the students just as much as the students needed the teachers.

One of my ideas in the drop-out prevention role was to create and operate a student-teacher mentor program for my STAAR students. The idea behind the mentor program was to establish a fun connection to school and academic success by building positive relationships with students, teachers and staff. I knew nothing about being a mentor and had very little knowledge on how to create a program that would connect students and instructors. But just as she saw my ability to lead, my principal believed I could pull this stunt off as well.

So I did what I felt was right in creating a program that would benefit both the student in need of a connection and the teacher in need of a reminder. Again, not having a clue as to how I was going to make this vision come to life, I pulled a list of students that fell into the criteria requested. I used the snapshots of each student and the information provided by the student to pair STAAR'S with a teacher. Once the snapshot pairing was complete, I sent an email introducing the program and invited

The Lesson Plan: An Educator's Inspiration

teachers to come participate in the schedule list of activities. For lack of a better phrase, it was a shot in the dark.

Teachers are already tasked with so many responsibilities. I feared I would not get the support from the teachers that would be necessary to make the program a success. From my experience as a classroom teacher, I knew the demands of the job made it hard to commit to extra activities. But I also remembered that the one thing my students loved was for me to sit down with them at lunch for a few minutes or have a conversation with them about an episode of a popular TV show or a new music video. As a teacher, all we want to do is make our students love the process of being educated. Deep down inside I knew that my fellow co-workers wanted the same for each and every student. Now with the change in leadership, the school's culture began to change. I no longer wondered if my colleagues liked kids, their willingness to help showed me they did. I even asked members of the administrative staff to join in and mentor students. Being the favorite student of an assistant principal or principal is certainly a new perspective for a student that is always in trouble or constantly being disciplined.

By the end of that same day most of my students and their mentor had committed to attending the first scheduled activity. Completely blown away by the response of the faculty, I stared at the wall and thought, "What now?" This mentor program was about to take off. Much sooner than I expected I would now have to plan to provide a meaning to the program. The first thought that came to mind was my memory of the mentor program I

The Lesson Plan: An Educator's Inspiration

was involved in as a high school student. Lame! I couldn't remember any event or conversation that made me want to rush and replicate that program. So I thought about it a little more. If teachers have reached out voluntarily to make a connection with a student, they probably had a personal connection to the students they selected.

As people, we associate ourselves to things and experiences that are shared with one another. Now, I could have been way off base, but I immediately assumed that my volunteers made a connection to the students the moment they saw them posted on the office wall. Maybe my volunteer teachers had an experience as a child that was similar to what my STAAR students were experiencing. With that assumption I vowed to make the extra time spent with students fun and memorable. I needed to take the staff back to a moment in their childhood, a moment that would lead to a connection with a troubled student.

After creating a plan of action based on the thought that former at-risk students were now helping current at-risk students, I decided to use fun as the tool to connect and motivate both my teachers and students. In order for students to connect to teachers, there would need to be a level of wackiness to take teachers and students out of their comfort zone. Themed monthly meetings provided laughter and an arena for students to see a different side of Mr. and Mrs. Classroom Teacher. Barefoot relay races, creating tie-dye t-shirts, and family photo swaps made it all come together. I made a point to feed and entertain the crowd all within a short 30 minute window. That was it, 30 minutes a month. In that 30 minutes we were able to establish connections that in turn would provide students with a new outlook on school and reward teachers for their dedications and commitment.

By the end of the semester, students that were not considered STAAR's were anxiously peeking in the cafeteria windows wondering how they could become a part of the program. The program even sparked the interest of a custodial staff member that I noticed observing the mentor program.

This friendly male custodian would always smile and wave to me as I conducted the monthly mentor meetings. Using the cafeteria as a meeting location, it was a routine pleasantry we exchanged. I never took the time to ask him if he would like to participate in the program. I just assumed he enjoyed the entertainment. I would later find the perfect match with this same custodian and a new student that was not fluent in the English language.

"Ms. Herald?" As I looked up to see a counselor and a young man standing in my office door way.

"Yes ma'am, I replied in a tone of urgency.

"I have a new student that is here from Cuba and it was suggested the he could benefit from the program you have created for some of the students."

As she stated the student's name and grade level, I couldn't help but to glance at the young man's shoes. By the time my eyes returned to the counselors head nod, the student was now taking a seat in my office and I was asked to give him a tour of his new surroundings. As he sat across from me, I shut down the computer and began to introduce myself again.

"I'm Ms. Herald, but I think you already know that," he shook his head and responded with a half-smile accepting my attempt to make him comfortable.

"I like your shoes, I said with a smile and thumbs up. "Retro 13's huh?"

He looked at me in awe and said in broken English,

"You wear Jordan's?"

"I do," I responded confidently.

Just then he reached to shake my hand with a huge grin as if we just made a deal on a used car lot. In that conversation about a popular brand of athletic shoes I made a genuine connection with a student.

"Ok, Ms. Herald" he said, almost to reassure our common bond.

We didn't say much else, but in that moment I became someone that he would recognize and associate with. As we walked past the cafeteria, we ran into my friendly custodian friend that had been observing the mentor program. Like always, he greeted me with a boisterous hello. As I replied, it dawned on me; my custodial friend would be the perfect mentor for this new student. As I introduced the two, I let the student know that he had just met the best custodian in the world and to seek him out if ever in need of help with his English or translation. They both smiled and agreed. I asked the custodian if he could stop by my office later because I was in need of a favor, turning away with a wink. He promised to come later that afternoon. After walking the new student to his class, I felt good about the connection that had just been established. This young man would now be a STAAR and I would have the opportunity to include an interested observer in the mentor program. Sure enough, the two attended the meetings and almost instantly the teachers were impressed that our loving custodian was now a mentor to a STAAR.

The next year I made sure to include this loving and thoughtful man that was once only viewed as a custodian. The mentor program gave him a purpose and a level of recognition that he would be admired for at the school and in the community. He made a promise to me that he would continue to assist and connect with students. I promised him that his positive involvement would be an example I would share with others. His participation in the program would be an innovative idea that I would never forget, even after I'd left that school site.

I would leave that position as Dropout Prevention Specialist at the end of my 5th year in education, but the thought of all the laughs and moments would never leave me. That year, I learned to continue to use everyday commonalities to make connections with both students and teachers. In addition, learning that overlooking an adult is the same as overlooking a child. Recognition and empowerment would be two frequently used strategies in my role as an administrator. As I was promoted to the next position, I reminisced on the times with the students and staff, allowing those moments to put things in perspective. At the end of the day we all are individuals that can be connected if we just recognize the mere presence of one another.

The Lesson Plan: An Educator's Inspiration
Leaders Empower
Seeking opportunities to empower others is a sign of leadership.

Don't be afraid to think outside of the box. Be on the lookout for individuals who are eager to help and take on additional tasks. Be receptive to feedback and suggestions from co-workers and staff. Also, don't be afraid to try new and unconventional suggested ideas.

As a teacher and administrator, utilize the help of volunteers in your community. There are people out there that want to help, they just have never been asked to do so.

Connect with a Purpose
When creating enrichment programs consider using everyone on your staff. In the narrative, I connected my custodian and student because I knew they

shared the same native language. Look at your staff and make connections that you know will benefit the student and potentially a staff member who is looking for a chance to make a difference.

Give a Little Time
Yet, there may not be additional pay available when committing to extra activities, the reward is priceless. When students know you are giving your free time to spend some time with them, they perceive you to be personable and caring. You may be the one person in their world that is taking time to support their goals.

Allow Your Teachers to be the Hero or Heroine
Teachers are natural heroes. If you are an administrator, allow your teachers and staff to help save the day. Ask them for help when planning and creating initiatives for students and other staff. Providing opportunities for your staff to give their feedback and ideas is also chance for them to display their talents. This allows the administration to sample a potential leader's contribution.

As a teacher, look to build relationships with people on site who teach the same subject area or grade level. Once those relationships have been established, ask for help. Sharing ideas and making improvements will ultimately strengthen everyone involved as educators.

K. L. Herald

The Lesson Plan

Chapter 6

Regularity Notice

The Lesson Plan: An Educator's Inspiration

You have probably heard someone make reference to the fact that kids have no filter. The words of kids are spoken with the utmost honesty and will leave you thinking well after the conversation is over. Working with students in a high school, I was surrounded by the non-filtered voices. Once I became an assistant principal, I started to listen to students more than I ever had before. Their indirect criticisms and nonchalant remarks made to me as I stood brainstorming during countless hours of lunch duty, lead me to reflect and question if I was living out my personal expectations for my own life.

Day in and day out in my career as a teacher and administrator, I repeatedly conveyed a message to students that promised a successful life through traits like hard work, dedication, a commitment to yourself, and a work ethic that would put the competition to rest. I talked about how to be successful. I felt like I was living a successful life and in many ways I felt I had arrived at the level in which I was encouraging my students to achieve. But the more and more I interacted with the students, I began to wonder if my presence and my current position in a high school had them convinced that education could lead to a lifetime of success. Now with 6 years of experience in education, I assumed that I had built somewhat of a level of credibility. It wasn't until a conversation with a student-athlete that I rescinded my "I have arrived" speech and began to question if I was truly exemplifying the testaments that I wanted my surrounding young minds to buy into.

    As a former high school basketball player I enjoy the sport and no matter what school site I am assigned to, I support the basketball teams. Having had an opportunity to be a student athlete, I find

The Lesson Plan: An Educator's Inspiration

myself being understanding to the challenge of balancing academics and athletics. When I was a young athlete, I remember having to make a commitment, play my role on the team, and work hard. All of the character traits I learned playing a game, became relevant to the reality of having a successful adult life. I attempted to mentor the student-athletes by sharing my personal challenges and triumphs from high school and college.

    This particular year I'd been introduced to a high school standout that was headed to the division I level of competition and was predicted to be a top athlete in college. She was an optimistic young lady to say the least. This kid not only was athletically gifted, she had an eye for fashion and aspirations of one day becoming a model. Something about her reminded me of my young student-athletes days. Every conversation with her left me asking myself if I was living up to my fullest potential. The level of confidence she exuded motivated me to improve in my own life and career. I probably had more conversations with her than any other student at the school because she was receptive to my advice, opinions, and encouragement. Or so I thought...

One day as we sat in my office we arrived on the topic of life after basketball and how I ended up as a high school administrator. I proceeded to provide a synopsis of my life story in all of 10 minutes and reiterated the fact that many athletes resort to professions such as teaching, coaching and public service after the final whistle blows.

"Not me," Ms. Basketball says to me in a convincing tone. "No offense but I don't want to be regular like you."

The Lesson Plan: An Educator's Inspiration

As I sat back in my chair with raised eyebrows I begged for her detailed description of what *regular* meant.

"I mean, you just work at a school. You have a regular house with a regular car and do regular things. I want more for my life. I don't want to end up being a regular person like you. No offense to you, but I want way more for my life."

Just as the words left her mouth the bell rung and she turned to walk out of my office leaving me with the most uncomfortable mixture of feelings similar to disgust and regret.

The rest of that day I moved in silence. I remember having a parent conference that afternoon and not remembering any of the concern that was brought into my office. I knew there was a parent in front of me that was pretty ticked off, but the entire meeting was like sitting in heavy fog.

Despite her loud tone and her choice of words, all I could hear were the words from the mouth of Ms. Basketball earlier in the day. When the dismissal bell rang that same afternoon, I grabbed my personal set of keys to my regular car and regular house. I closed the door to the office of the regular school which I had spent my time that day. With a careless attitude I neglected to pack up my calendar or workload that I usually took home to complete in the evenings. I walked through the crowd of students that were milling about in front of the school and made my way in between the buses and past the parent pick-up line to my car. I arrived at my house and in all honesty looking back, I don't even remember driving there. I opened my front door, took one step inside and fell to my knees causing the door to shut behind me. Talk about a moment of self-reflection. At that moment I began to ask myself a plethora of questions, with the first one being 'at what point did I lose sight of my own dreams?'

Through the tears coming down my face I looked around at the walls in my house to see photos of my youth and early adult life. I immediately started trying to piece together my journey hoping to find an answer to the many questions I had for myself. With no consolation I had no explanation or solid reasoning for where I was at that moment in my life.

I lay on the floor, closed my eyes and muttered into the space surrounding me, "God put me here for a reason." I must have fallen asleep and woke up long enough to make it to my bedroom. When the alarm clock rang at the set time of 5:45am, it was time to return to my regular job.

As a teacher, you have an enormous responsibility. The majority of a child's time is spent at school. Most students spend anywhere between 35-40 hours a week with their teachers. The safety and instruction of someone's child is in your hands. In order to convey a message that positively builds a child's character you plan, dress appropriately, and speak using the most compassionate language known to man. There are times when you have to use your own money to purchase materials for your students to ensure their academic success. Sometimes you will not be supported when you think of a creative way to motivate or instruct your students. You experience overcrowded classrooms with some students that could care less about being at school. Many teachers prepare during unpaid hours, including the weekends. Your entire mission is to educate and prepare a child for their future. If you are lucky, you may see that student years later when they pop up to visit you or one day run into them in the grocery store. More often than not, you don't get the privilege of seeing just what your hard work and efforts produced.

As an administrator, you struggle to balance a level of professionalism and compassion. Your main objective is not only to ensure the safety and supervision of the students, you also have a staff to protect. You not only protect the physical well-being of your teachers, you protect them as professionals when parents and students attempt to disregard their teaching strategies and level of professionalism. Your job is to reinforce the practice of productive student learning, all while enforcing ethical workplace behavior. None of which is an easy thing to do.

The profession of educating is more than a regular job. I compare the words from a teacher's mouth to the delicate hands of a brain surgeon. You have chosen to shape a human life. Shaping a child's life through communication, encouragement, challenging their level of thought, interacting and modeling the correct words and behaviors; it's what an educator does. I feel confident in saying that educating others is necessary and takes a level of precision that is perfected through repetition and time. In education, there are no two days alike and with extensive planning and preparation you can never predict the day ahead.

The conversation with Ms. Basketball broke me down. Realistically, I knew that her words were not intentionally meant to be disrespectful or hurtful. She had just given me a friendly reminder that as long as you're living, it's not too late to work towards dreams and goals. Having the belief that everything in this world happens for a reason, the conversation propelled me to seek out my own strengths and

The Lesson Plan: An Educator's Inspiration

talents. Counting the conversations with her and hundreds of other students, there was evidence that I was positively impacted students. Reaching students, teachers and parents was my gift. Coincidentally, that day's conversation sparked me to take my talents to a whole new level and encouraged me expand my reach as an educator to others beyond my community and school site.

My former students may be surprised to hear this, but I have been inspired by some of their words and actions towards me. I could go on to name student after student that encouraged the writing of this inspirational book. My students ended up being my teachers. The lessons they taught me caused me to review my professional level and triggered me to prove that education is extremely important. The regular life I had chosen would not only change me, it would eventually transform others into so much more.

The Lesson Plan: An Educator's Inspiration
Teachers and School Administrators are Important

The decision to teach means that you will have direct influence in someone's life. The way you speak, discipline and instruct a child could leave an impact that will last a lifetime. Teachers are vital to a child's growth and intellectual development. The profession of teaching is not just an ordinary job. You are expected to do the extraordinary.

Teamwork, Dedication, and Hard Work

If you have ever played an organized sport or been a part of a team, you are familiar with teamwork, dedication to that team and hard work. If you are an athlete or at some point in your life played a sport, bring your experience as an athlete into your daily teaching strategies. Use examples that relate to sports to motivate and encourage student participation. Also, creating teams in your class provides an element of competition that can potentially motivate students to achieve academic success.

You are a Salesperson for Education

As a teacher or school administrator you are a salesperson for education. You not only have to teach and guide a child in your role as a teacher or school educator, you have to be convincing as well. Show your students the importance and rewards of being educated. Display your own diploma or certificates of accomplishment in your classroom or office. Explain to students the progression from grade level to graduation and beyond. Tell students the requirements to becoming qualified for a teaching position or other careers. Providing direct examples informs students of the steps that need to be taken to achieve their goals.

Don't Lose Sight of Your Own Goals Along the Way...

Remember, you are a professional but you are also a human being with interest, needs and wants. If you have a goal or dream that keeps you up at night, go for it. If it means that you put a plan in place or extend your timeline to reach your goal, make the moves necessary no matter what.

Schedule short periods of time during the week that will allow you the opportunity to focus on your plan. I set aside 1 hour a week for writing when I initially started working towards publishing this work. The hour wasn't much time, but the hours spent definitely added up and the project was completed.

The Lesson Plan

Chapter 7

Stand Up and Stand Out

The fact is, it isn't easy being a young educator or administrator. When many people on the school's faculty and staff have several more years of experience, you start to question your own capabilities as a professional. Walking into a setting where my immediate battle was to gain respect as a leader and as an educator was challenging. I wanted to be respected and viewed as a leader by the older and more experienced staff. In my heart I believed that I possessed something special that did not require a certain age or experience requirement. As I walked the campus, I realized what set me apart from the more experienced educator. I knew my purpose in this world is to educate and motivate. I felt overcome with a genuine enthusiasm and interest to inspire others. I cared about planning a faculty recognition event or celebrating school wide accomplishments more than anything else.

The Lesson Plan: An Educator's Inspiration

Being an administrator paid my bills, being able to encourage others to their highest level of potential made me rich. By no means did my employment afford me a lavish lifestyle. The payment I received from my faculty, staff, students and even parents was in the form of accomplishment and achieved goals. It was the confirmation that I had the gift to empower others.

This revelation came to me when I realized that the staff was generously assisting and contributing energy to produce results. The people that worked for me began to work with me to fulfill the vision and mission of the school site. The group of students and staff in return motivated me to reach more individuals and to create and accomplish more goals. In time, that same group of people that surpassed me with experience, were now looking to me as a leader. It only required that I humble myself and speak to what I was most passionate about; bringing out the best in others.

An effective leader is continually seeking opportunities to strengthen and encourage the individuals that are following them. The catch phrase, "you are only as strong as you weakest link" holds merit in regards to a faculty of school teachers. As I observed both administrators and classroom teachers, I noticed a correlation between successful teachers and administrators. The teachers and administrators that encouraged and brought positive momentum to others made a difference in the overall culture of the school. Teachers respond positively to encouragement and motivation, just as students do. Just like a troubled and unsuccessful student, a struggling teacher needs a little extra

The Lesson Plan: An Educator's Inspiration

motivation to be successful. Even in our roles as professionals, many times we need to be reminded of our capabilities; almost as a confirmation that we are able to produce and perform. I myself was included in this group of educators in need of encouragement. To my surprise, just as I observed teachers on a daily basis, they were in return observing me.

Well into the semester I completed several informal classroom observations and made friendly thumbs up visits to my teachers to give them a glimpse of encouragement. With over 100 teachers on staff, I had no defined system in regards to whom and where I visited during the school day. Typically I would just walk the hall and grab the door handle that was within reach during my trek. On this particular day I walked into a Spanish classroom that for some reason or other I had not made an appearance in this school year. I did my normal routine of gently entering the room as to avoid a disruption that would cause the students to veer off task. I slid to an area in the back of the room, as I did in most cases, and made eye contact with the teacher. He smiled and I smiled back. I crossed my hands in front of my waist and gave clues to indicate that I did not need to speak to him at that moment. I was just there to visit.

As I stood there and took note of this gentleman, I was impressed. He was older, maybe around 55 or so. He himself was of Hispanic descent and his dress reminded me of a cigar lounge owner I had once seen on the cover of a Spanish textbook. He held the attention of his students and they responded to his commands. He then gave instruction for the students to complete an individual task and began to walk in my direction. As I stood in a respectful stance and awaited his approach I leaned in to prepare for his anticipated whisper, as he was much shorter than me.

"I almost thought you forgot about me, "he said to me with a slightly shaken voice.

Stunned I replied, "I'm sorry sir, what do you mean."

He looked up and smiled and began to state that he was anxiously waiting for me to visit and see him in action. He extended his statement to describe conversations he heard from other faculty members and their feeling of reassurance and recognition that my visits left behind. I shook his hand and apologized.

"I didn't realize what I was missing out on." I whispered back with a wink and a smile.

At that moment I received the affirmation that my efforts were being positively received. My faculty and staff depended on me. That experience with him proved that recognition was necessary to keep teachers motivated despite the difficulty of their job. Finding the time to circulate the campus and support teachers is a requirement of the job, but at times is difficult to do. With the remarks I received from him, I had just been paid in full for making the effort.

As a teacher, invite your administration in your classroom to see just what is going on. When possible, post pictures and videos on your school's internal communication system of student work or activities. This will allow your colleagues to see all the good things that are happening. The use of social media can also provide an avenue for you to broadcast your teaching strategies. Webinars and podcast are a good way to make instruction available and convenient to your students. When parents are able to access materials and electronic resources to assist their student, the level of parent involvement increases. With your instruction readily available, students have a greater chance of academic success.

As an administrator, remember that teachers perform their best when they are encouraged and recognized. Teachers and staff want the support of their administrative staff. If you have teachers on your staff that are utilizing technology to broadcast their instructional strategies, share the idea with your entire faculty. Compliments are valuable to teachers and others members on staff. When I was a classroom teacher, I wanted my leadership team to see just how much I enjoyed my job. I wanted them to know that I had a level of confidence in what I was doing. Being a visible administrator on your campus can motivate your staff and improve your students' academic success. Teachers want to know that their school leadership is supporting their efforts to achieve the same goal; student enrichment and achievement.

As I closed the door to that Spanish class in the same manner that I had opened it, I vowed to be visual, smile and make it a daily objective to support my staff and attend their performances as much as possible.

The Lesson Plan: An Educator's Inspiration
Be Visible
Being physically present has the same effect for both a teacher and an administrator. Just as a student will be less likely to misbehave if a teacher is present, a teacher will be more likely to display professionalism and work to leave an impression in the presence of a supervisor.

Teachers, assist by standing at your doors or being in the hallways during student circulation. The more supervision the less likely student horseplay or physical altercation will occur.

For administrators, many issues that come from students and teachers being unsupervised can be avoided if a system of circulation is established. Set up a rotation with your leadership staff that allow for administrative presence throughout the school.

Sell Yourself
Teachers, prioritize making the success of both you and your students known. In large schools, the

administration may only get to see your talent a few times a year. Use technology to capture your best moments. Don't be afraid to share those moments. Today, we all are looking for instantaneous results. Being able to show a potential employer a portfolio of your teaching in the form of video, photos and web images makes you marketable as an educator.

The Lesson Plan

Chapter 8

Conflict of Interest

Familiarity with one's own ego is the trick to understanding how to accommodate the ego of others. In my professional journey, learning how to respond to the various personalities that I came in contact with on a daily basis was not easy. Leadership encompasses several components. Often in a leadership role you are responsible for making difficult decisions. When making difficult decisions, ideally you want to be supported by surrounding leaders that are presumed to share the mission and vision. There were times when I felt like my decisions were not supported by my surrounding administrative team. Feeling alone and unsupported is the most uncomfortable feeling causing unnecessary feelings of despair and regret.

It's not uncommon for decisions to be challenged by co-workers and stakeholders. But when your team doesn't support you, it can make you feel worthless. When being assertive as a leader you will often be forced to stand up and make a tough decision and sometimes you will be supporting that decision alone. For me, I quickly learned that one of the most significant components of holding a leadership position is the element of trust.

As a young educator and leader, there is a level of competition amongst your peers that deters the natural ability for individuals to form a common bond of loyalty and trust. At the onset of being appointed to one of the most challenging roles in my professional career several revelations surfaced. I was one of the youngest candidates, had very few years' experience as a leader, and was not currently on the school's staff when interviewing for the position. Knowing very little about the position, I feared that if I didn't challenge myself professionally, forever being stuck in the trenches of discipline and bus duty would be my destiny. Applying for the position and familiarizing myself with the workings of this inner city high school took precedent. I researched the necessary information and prepared to complete the interview process. I was interviewed by a panel of what was comprised of site's leadership to analyze if my skills and experience fit the needs of the school. I knew going into the position that I was not the number one candidate. Nevertheless, I was confident that I could do the job. After a month of waiting for a call I was appointed to the position.

Once in the position I began to feel the pressure of being the new kid on the block. It wasn't long into my role that I was introduced to the concept of trust and loyalty within a leadership staff. Trust is necessary for a group to obtain any head-way in the midst of achieving a common goal. Now, keeping in mind that working with others was a personal strength, working with others who failed to recognize and accept my contribution was a bit more challenging. There were days when I wanted to hand over my duties and responsibilities and say with a smile, "It's all yours." There were times when I was called out in staff meetings for mistakes made due to my unfamiliarity in the new role. Any positive and productive initiatives that I presented seemed to be apathetically received. I felt as if I was in a constant race with no finish line in sight. With the deck being stacked against me in regards to being young and new to the site, I purposely worked harder to gain credibility.

I can recall instances when teachers purposely overlooked me in my role because I was not the individual they felt deserved the position. I needed someone to trust. I needed someone that would inform me prior to my screw up and defend me every step of the way.

Trusting others is something that most career driven individuals lack. The constant pressure to perform and seek promotion makes it almost impossible to depend on others. I questioned the motives of everyone around me. I shut down even at the slightest informal conversation in fear that my openness would be used to aid in the demise of my career. A relaxed and genuine hello was never given to anyone within my direct leadership circle for most of my first year in my new position. I couldn't allow myself to relax or open up to an unfamiliar group.

The Lesson Plan: An Educator's Inspiration

Eventually I grew to dislike the person I was becoming. I closed myself off and turned off my shining spirit that had provided all the opportunities in my life thus far. Being unhappy is toxic and that was one word I did not want to be communicated in reference to me and my character.

Over the course of working at this new job site the words, fun and loving were replaced with silent and stern. One stressful day I walked into the office and stood speechless in front of my secretary's desk. I had nothing to say and no energy to complete another task. I'd just left a staff meeting in which members of my leadership team transmitted text messages that were of obvious humor while I was speaking on issues that affected our student body. My secretary could see that I was at the verge of complete meltdown. The words that she spoke to me changed my mindset completely and I began to feel a sense of relief.

She sat up straight, looked me dead in the eye and said, "The difference between you and everyone else is that this position is not a job for you. This assignment that you have been given is your purpose."

I stared back at her and said, "I'm listening."

"When you accept this job as your purpose, your validation will not come from the daily struggle. Don't expect others to congratulate you or encourage you, that just doesn't happen all the time. You will be rewarded through your efforts to genuinely help others."

In that moment my whole outlook on my position shifted from being a prison sentence, to my calling. The disrespectful laughter from those who were supposed to be on my "team" did not harm my emotional state. In effect, I welcomed the laughter as an invitation to continue doing my best. I had to be genuine to myself and let my spirit radiate onto others. I slowly began to trust the process of being genuine to others in hopes that they recognized me as a hard working component to the leadership circle. Displaying dedication to my team and our school wide vision allowed me to think forwardly. I stepped out of my comfort zone of cancelling out ones who I felt couldn't clearly be trusted and started a method of professional communication. I asked questions like, "Can I get your help?" That was one step in giving others an opportunity to either help or disappoint me…hoping for a positive outcome. Shifting from a fear of being embarrassed to allowing others to either show good or bad character begin to take the weight off of me. I stopped looking for individuals to trust, I began to trust that knowing who I was as a leader was enough to carry me through and provide continued success. I made a conscious effort to not allow the demands of my life to prevent me from my original intention to lead by example and motivate.

The process of focusing on my own dreams overshadowed my fear of falling short of the expectations created by the people around me. Viewing my job as my purpose was powerful in shaping my role as a leader. No longer would I concentrate on convincing others around me that I was a competent leader. I realized that the steps of my journey had been planned just for me. The challenges were building my character as a leader; building another part of my professional toolkit.

It took some time for me to accept that not everyone will be convinced of my abilities. Regardless of what was happening around me, I had a job to do. The intention wasn't for me to gain approval from others. Leading with an honest and hardworking approach would be recognized by the individuals that appreciated just that, honesty and hard work. I put my trust in my faith and worked to be the best leader I could possibly be.

The Lesson Plan: An Educator's Inspiration
Get to Know Your Team
It's important to know who you are working with. Knowing the strengths and weaknesses of your surrounding team allows you to complete each other as a whole. Take time to get to know one another before and after tackling an important task. Try asking questions like,

- Are you comfortable with this type of task?

- What experience have you had with...?
- What role would you like to have in...?
- Are you good at...?
- Do you prefer...?
- What do you think we could have done differently?

We cannot just assume in a room full of leaders that we all come to the table with the same experience and mindset.

Healthy Competition

Motivating and encouraging one another to improve is what leaders do best. When working with co-workers, remember to think of ways to help one another improve professionally. Try giving a task to a co-worker who is assigned a different job role. This provides an opportunity for that individual to expand his or her professional toolkit and you to display your leadership abilities. If we are never pushed to be our best, how will we ever know what we are capable of accomplishing?

Lead at Your Level

The element of collaboration can sustain any obstacle especially when others are willing to admit their own strengths and weaknesses. Know what you are good at and be ok with admitting the things you are not. Trust that your team will step up when you unprepared for the challenge. Learn as much as you can and help when you have the tools to do so.

Stick to the Common Goal

The assurance of knowing that each member of the team is focused on the same goal makes the group effective. Dedicate yourself to that goal and support others around as you all work together.

You Can Do It

Good intentions and hard work can often surpass the most talented of individuals. Be confident in your job role and always look for opportunities to grow within that role. If you don't believe in yourself, how can anyone else? Avoid doubting yourself at all cost.

Understanding Different Leadership Styles

Learning about different leadership styles can help you identify what type of leader you are and how you want to be lead. When knowing who you are as a leader, you have a self-awareness that can help prevent conflicts with others along the way.

The Lesson Plan

Chapter 9

Driven by Faith

K. L. Herald

Your mindset in the midst of trying times is based on what you believe. Whatever you believe in or the source of your faith is the advantage you have over others. For me, the belief in God is how I am able to make it in this profession. As you walk in the steps that are pre-determined for you, others may not understand that you are living out your calling and not just working at a job.

There were times that others just couldn't understand how I could hold my head high after the most tumultuous moment. I've lost track of the number of times someone in the office has asked me the most frequently asked question, Are you alright? One afternoon while sitting in my office I overheard a conversation with a student and another adult that involved the student missing the bus. I thought nothing of it because a student missing the bus is something that happens daily at a school. About 15 or 20 minutes later I hear a parent yelling at the top of her lungs.

"I want to talk to the coward that put my baby on the phone to tell me that she missed the bus!" The parent was livid. "I'm sick of this school and how they treat the students here," she went on to say.

The parent went on for a few minutes and I myself wondered who was the last adult assisting the child. I immediately got up from my desk and approached the parent.

"Ma'am, would you like to step inside my office? I would be more than happy to assist you." I spoke in a calming tone trying to convince this mom that I was genuinely concerned.

"No, I don't want to talk to you. I want to talk to the coward that was afraid to call me!"

I stood at the door to my office, crossed my hands in front of my lap and said to the parent, "Ma'am, I was the person that called you. If you allow me the opportunity, I would love to speak with you in private."

The parent walked into my office with a swiftness that illustrated her next step would be choking me for sure.

There were several people in the office and their eyes grew as wide as baseballs when I invited this irate parent into the confinements of my office; which was the size of gas station bathroom. As she stepped into my office I shut the door behind me and motioned for her to sit down. My office phone immediately began to ring and I ignored the call that was coming from my secretary outside the door. Again, I motioned for her to sit as I stepped behind my desk to begin to resolve the issue.

"I don't want to sit down. I'm pissed off," she sharply stated.

I replied understanding her anger and proceeded to have a seat behind my desk. I said nothing. I listened to the parents' concerns. I was receiving the verbal punishment that she wanted to give the last person that instructed her child to call her. I sat quietly, unshaken and allowed her to unleash her opinion and frustration all over me. As time went on she began to calm down and decided to have a seat. When I was able to speak, I complimented her on being such an involved and supportive parent. I told her that I was thankful to see how thoroughly concerned she was with the well-being of her child. I reassured her that I took my position as an educator seriously and that I made it a priority to treat each child as my own. I apologized for the miscommunication and put a plan in place to avoid this occurrence in the future. As I began to see the storm subside in her eyes, I reached to the corner of my desk and slid a small bible to the center between me and her. She looked down at the bible and I looked directly in her eyes.

"I lied to you ma'am," I said in a tone of forgiveness. "I was not the person that called you earlier this afternoon. But as I sat behind my desk hearing how upset you were, I knew it was my responsibility to address your concerns immediately. I knew you would not allow me to help you if I didn't take the blame. So I took ownership of something I did not do. I lied to you."

At that moment the conversation took a total turn. Her pride wouldn't allow her to compliment me for what I believed to be a brave measure. But her faith allowed her to say,

"We need more believers in the schools now-a-days", she said firmly with her hands crossed at her chest.

As she sat back and allowed a half smile surface on her face, I knew I'd made the right decision that afternoon.

Her actions confirmed that she understood me. She saw my purpose and she was relieved. As I extended my hand to meet hers, I reaffirmed my purpose and welcomed her to return directly to me the next time she had a problem. When I opened the door, the same staff was standing by. All took a deep breath as they stood anxiously waiting for the now calm and satisfied parent to exit. When the coast was clear my secretary rushed in my office and said with a smile on her face,

"The other secretary wanted me to call and make sure you were okay. But I wasn't worried about you. You carry a shield of protection around you and the right words are always placed on the tip of your tongue."

I smiled and humbly returned to what I was doing before the incident occurred. It wasn't the first time I encountered that type of situation and I was sure it wouldn't be the last.

The Lesson Plan: An Educator's Inspiration

    Moments of anger and frustration like this occur all the time. As a teacher and educational leader you have to know that you have been placed and prepared for such challenges. Just as children are taught right from wrong, we as adults know when we are out of line. I never raised my voice to the parent and I allowed her the opportunity to vent. Most importantly, I listened.

    The Bible was not presented as a reminder of her behavior. It was a reminder to me, to own up to what I had done wrong, which was lying to the parent. It wasn't my fault that the child missed the bus. There was nothing I could do to change what happened early that afternoon. All I could do was take responsibility for what I had done. Having faith that I would receive support to handle the situation, I owned it. A leader is expected to take the lead. As I did just that, the parent followed.

As a teacher, you are not able to openly discuss religion or your beliefs. Fortunately, there is no restriction on using those beliefs in your daily life. Whatever you refer to as a source of faith, use it to keep you balanced as an individual and professional. When working with others, allow the principles of your heart and mind to support your decision making.

As an administrator, the responsibility to oversee each component of a school site requires that you have a genuine interest for others. Evidence of your faith base will not only determine how your following views you as a leader, it will ultimately be modeled by others who are observing your leadership style.

As people that have daily contact with others of various cultures, genders, religions and backgrounds; using faith as a resource to cope with problems can make a difference as you grow personally and professionally. Whatever you believe in, make sure your faith is an important and frequently used instrument in your professional toolkit.

The Lesson Plan: An Educator's Inspiration
Have Faith

There will be good days and bad days. Prayer helped me when things weren't going so well. If you depend on your faith to assist you and guide your life, it's ok. If taking a few minutes during the day to refocus yourself with the use of prayer or reading inspirational material as your coping mechanism, make time for it.

Allow Your Principles to Lead You

Your display of faith and the behaviors you exhibit from your beliefs can show others what your intentions are. You don't have to disclose your religion or faith to everyone you meet. Hopefully, through your actions and words your principles will surface and your compassion for others will be noticed.

Making Faith-Based Connections

When having faith and struggles in common, you have someone that understands exactly what you are going through and the way you prefer to deal with your problems. Make faith based connections with your co-workers. Those same connections can be used to help you survive the challenges in your profession each and every day.

The Lesson Plan

Chapter 10

Strengthen the Focus

K. L. Herald

The most profound strategy I gained for my professional toolkit was to remain direct, stick to the facts, and let every word you speak come from your passion to assist and protect others. When having difficult conversations, the person you are speaking to must know that your statements are coming from a genuine place and are focused on the overall mission and goal. Many professionals want to be informed on their job performance, especially from their immediate supervisors. While training under experienced leaders I was taught to balance positive recognition with areas of concern. This balance makes your feedback more effective. Sooner than I expected I would have to pull this tool out and put it into practice. Being young and new to my position, I wanted my staff to know their value and the possibility for them to grow professionally. Feeling this way left me with no choice but to demonstrate my knowledge as an experienced leader and conduct myself as one.

Annual evaluations are typical in any profession. Usually a supervisor or member of upper management is responsible for reviewing the performance of employees placed under their supervision. Given the responsibility of evaluating assistants and support staff, I wanted to provide a form of feedback that could be used to support overall job improvement. When planning meetings to discuss the annual observation rubric, I created a form that would provide employees with both areas of strength and areas that they would need to focus on for the upcoming year. My whole thought process was centered on educating and empowering the employee.

One of my scheduled evaluation meetings was for a gentleman on staff that had a great rapport with students, was a hard worker and a member of the staff for almost 19 years. When I compared his performance with the evaluation form, the only area of concern was his tardiness to work on several occasions. As I prepared to meet with him, I built the conversation around the many positive attributes he had as a member of the staff. I not only wanted to make him aware of his contributions, I needed him to see the influential impact he had on students; both positive and negative.

"Good morning" I expressed cheerfully as the staff member sat down on the other side of my desk.

"Good morning", he stated apprehensively.

The Lesson Plan: An Educator's Inspiration

From his mannerism I could tell that he was anxious to hear my feedback and didn't want to waste time with formalities. As I pulled the evaluation form out of a folder we both leaned in to see the comparison of remarks on the paper. As I reviewed each standard I provided feedback to the staff member to support how he was evaluated. I supported my response with actual events including dates.

"Let me begin by pointing out a couple of the many strengths you have as a member of our staff". I could see his demeanor switch from worry to interest.

I pointed out a few strong points and supported those points with examples of when the strength was displayed. The evidence presented the staff member a compliment that was direct and factual. With the strategy of identifying what the staff member was great at, I could easily open the conversation up to discuss what could be improved for the upcoming year.

"One area I would like to see you concentrate on is the willingness to take initiative in building upon some of the strengths we just discussed." I said as the gentlemen looked at me with a look of confusion.

"You have such a great rapport with the students, you could establish a greater connection if you modeled the punctuality that you expect from them." As he shook his head and agreed with me, I knew he was self-reflecting on his professional punctuality. In that statement I made the area of improvement known and I also attached why improvement in the area of punctuality was important.

The Lesson Plan: An Educator's Inspiration

"You know ma'am, I didn't realize the negative effect being late to duty had. The last thing I would want is the kids to justify their own tardiness by my actions," he stated in a moment of realization.

We put a timeline in place and agreed to have a conversation at a later date to review his progress.

We shook hands and as he walked to my office door he turned and said, "Thank you. In all my years working in this county I have never had anyone to personally tell me what I was good and bad at."

I smiled and said, "You are very welcome." It seemed as if he was almost happy to find out how he could improve as a staff member.

As an employee, I know how it feels to be in fear of losing your job or position. We as people all want to be recognized for doing something well. We as people also want to know when something isn't right so we can fix it.

As a teacher, be willing to hear what you can improve to become the best possible teacher in the profession. Challenge your administrator or supervisor to give you an area of focus each year. Even if your observations or evaluations state that you are doing well as a classroom teacher, always look for areas to improve. Asking for areas to improve on is an indication to your leadership team that you take your role as a teacher seriously. It is also an indication that you want to grow professionally. Some teachers even identify areas they feel need improvement and willingly ask for suggestions on how to make changes in their classrooms.

The Lesson Plan: An Educator's Inspiration

As an administrator or leadership staff, take time to provide your staff with solid examples of how to improve in their profession. Be direct and give suggestions. Give your teachers and staff the opportunity to improve. Remind your teachers that the overall objective is to effectively educate the students. Be honest and state what you would like the employee to do to improve. Many times, we fail to provide the individual with the exact steps necessary to be successful in the role. Just as teachers need to give specific steps to students, administrators must provide the necessary steps for teachers to have professional success.

The Lesson Plan: An Educator's Inspiration
Difficult Conversations Must Happen

As a professional, be confident when speaking and use actual data to lead difficult conversation. I found it much easier to address the problem when sticking to the data and evidence. When possible, provide a copy of the data to the other person or people so they can also review it.

Happy Endings Aren't Guaranteed

Of course we all want every conversation to end with all parties leaving the room happy about the decision that was made. Unfortunately, there will be times when all parties agree to disagree and no resolution is established. Know that the decision you made was made in good judgment. Keep the overall goal and mission in mind.

As a teacher or employee working with another staff members, try to focus your concerns on the impact the problem has in relation to the overall goal or mission. When attempting to resolve a conflict, make reference to how a solution can positively impact the students, school or surrounding community. Try to get the staff member or members to formulate their own solution that works well for all parties involved. This way the decision is a collaborative effort and less of a directive.

As an administrator, stick to factual evidence or data as the objective of the conversation. Have the data on hand to review with the employee and allow feedback as part of the discussion. Emphasize the importance of your concern by using examples of how the problem is effecting your students or school. Remind the employee of their role and the expectations within that role.

Balance the Positive and the Negative

The technique of balancing strength and weakness helps the other person be more receptive. Complimenting your fellow teacher before stating the problem lets that person know they are not a complete failure. Highlighting individual contributions to the organization gives that person a sense of belonging and ownership. Try to use terms such as *area of improvement* or *suggested idea/strategy* when problem solving. A positive tone can have an effect.

Emphasize the Big Picture
Make reference to the overall goal. For educators, the primary objective is educating and providing safety to all students. In a school setting, ultimately every decision is made in the best interest of the students. Every conversation must revert back to what is best for kids.

The Lesson Plan

Chapter 11

Value Source

K. L. Herald

As a teacher or aspiring teacher, you probably have an idea as to what type of teacher you want to be known as. You probably think about your own experience as a student sitting in the class of your favorite teacher. Most people can recite stories of what they remember their favorite teacher doing or saying. That teacher you can easily remember hopefully left a positive effect on you and a positive perception of themselves.

For example, you may want to be known for your witty personality and your will to support students in the classroom and in the community. You may want to be the teacher that is always there in the nick of time to assist with behavior problems or issues that are not totally related to school. You may possess a natural mother or father like love for kids that is welcoming and provides a sense of security.

The Lesson Plan: An Educator's Inspiration

Whatever your personality may be, use it as a way of setting yourself apart from others in the profession. Making yourself special and showcasing your character encourages students to do the same. Being able to provide more than just the curriculum to your student's is your value as an education professional.

Information is so accessible today; students want to know what you as an educator can provide them that they can't access within seconds from the internet. Many classroom teachers find that behavior management is a struggle more so than years past because the needs and interest of the students have changed so drastically. With other avenues that are available for students to complete secondary and post-secondary requirements, the traditional in-class style of teaching is slowly losing its appeal. The student now has a choice in how they want to be educated. The reality of societal trends places emphasis on the value of the classroom teacher. The challenge for the classroom teacher now is to plan and create a teaching method that will hold the students interest and keep the students wanting more; from you and only you as that teacher for that specific subject. As teachers, we must change our mindset to believe that we possess a special gift that can only be given from us individually.

This shift occurred to me one afternoon as a group of three boys ran past me in the courtyard. After my request to stop running went from a simple statement to a demand, the boys stopped in their tracks for me to question them.

"We run through the halls now?" I asked the boys with a raised eyebrow. Being familiar with me and my word choice at times, the boys laughed a little but still seemed to be in a hurry. The looked at me with half smiles and apologized but begged to provide an explanation.

"It's Thursday and Mrs. Walker always tells us who will be the student of the week. That person also gets to take her place and gets to teach the last 15 minutes of class period."

"We even get to do a personal presentation on ourselves." Another young man in the group added.

Listening to the young men's excitement almost made me want to apologize for stopping them. They were being motivated and challenged by a teacher. Ms. Walker was adding a personalized element in her class that only she could provide. That personal level of recognition was getting her students to buy into what she was doing. Not only were the student's being recognized, they were given an opportunity to learn leadership skills.

As I released the young men to proceed to Ms. Walker's class I noticed another group of kids that were not making any effort to get to class. Without even speaking to the group of lingering students, I turned and headed in the direction of Ms. Walker's classroom. I needed to recognize her for what she was doing and I needed her to share it with others on our staff.

The Lesson Plan: An Educator's Inspiration

Teachers

There is no instruction manual that tells you how to let your personality assist you as an educator. You don't need one. Be who you are and don't be afraid to let your personality shine through. You are a performer with an audience filled with students, teachers, parents and administrators. All eyes are on you. Show them all that you are more than a teacher. Show them that you are **THE** teacher and what you have to teach cannot be found on the World Wide Web.

Something in your actions, way of dress, or attitude may influence a fellow co-worker to do the same. Don't feel as if your co-workers are copying or stealing your style. Remember, when someone copies what you have done it is a form of flattery. If the end result is student achievement and success of the overall school, then you are definitely providing a positive example.

Administrators

During my career I can honestly say that I have been fortunate to work with leaders that have positively influenced me to one day assume a leadership role. In my 8 years in education, I was lucky enough to be supervised by several distinct leadership styles. From each of my supervisors I learned strategies to add to my professional toolkit. When you aspire to be an educational leader, be mindful in selecting role models that will teach you the tools that will lead to your effectiveness. The smartest strategy when selecting a leader is to survey the opinion of others under their leadership. If an overwhelming majority of effective staff members faithfully sing praises about the respected leader, he or she may need to become your immediate example of what leadership should look like. Also, if you are lucky enough to catch up with a leader on the fast track, keep an eye on the way they move. You may be able to grasp techniques that could potential propel you forward in your own career. Take notes and always place what you learn in your own professional toolkit.

The Lesson Plan

Chapter 12

Self-Motivation

Motivating yourself when no one else is around can be a challenge for some people. It may sound simple to establish a personal protocol for picking yourself off of the ground. In reality, it's more difficult to do than say. Think about it, if you knew how to prevent yourself from dropping to the lowest point of discouragement you wouldn't be there in the first place. Many times we just can't locate the inner strength to get up and put the pieces together to move forward. You have probably seen this happen to someone on your faculty or staff that just couldn't bounce back to a level of return. Not everyone at your site has the same challenges. The chance of one solution being the answer for everyone's problem is nearly impossible. What works for one person could or wouldn't work for someone else. It would be great if we all worked where there were no problems and everyone on staff was happy and loved what they did for a living. Somewhere this could be the case, but from my experience it doesn't happen too often.

Regrettably, not all teachers and administrators are working at sites for school districts that provide a promising and motivating work environment. This is where the challenge arises. Adult life has a tendency to strip the act of living from our mind and spirit. Working in education is mentally exhausting, in both roles as a teacher and administrator. In the course of 8 years there have been moments of reluctance, exhaustion, and lack of enthusiasm. The same feelings lead me to focus on the importance of intrinsic motivation.

As a teacher, don't be afraid to celebrate your own success. Your example of recognizing your own success lets your student's know that it's okay for them to do the same. Pat yourself on the back when necessary. Keep record of your professional achievements that can be accessed by others who inquire. Teach the character traits of pride and confidence to your students. Celebrating any accomplishment leaves a memory that drives you towards the next achievement. Live in the mindset that you are good at what you do, but you are also working to become even better.

As an administrator you are constantly solving the all the problems while being harassed by some and being disappointed by others. You try day in and day out to maintain the momentum to encourage and extinguish fires simultaneously. Sometimes the school site seems as a battlefield and the goal of reaching a collective vision, the war. So despite your exhaustion, a leader isn't given a moments rest. Knowing that you will be the last man or woman standing, you have to prepare for producing your best work under the most trying circumstances. Excuses from leaders aren't necessarily appealing. The most notable leaders can console, direct, reprimand, and problem solve all at the drop of a hat. You learn the key to being a leader is to take a deep breath, regain composure and perform. You pull the intrinsic reward of being the lead performer in the show out from your heart and mind.

Many times teachers and administrators will never disclose setbacks to the staff. Just as teachers sometimes delay information to students and parents don't divulge problems to their children, we try to fix things and make it all go away. In the lead role as administrator, teacher and parent we are seeking to do what's best for our staff, students and family. When you struggle to conjure up enough strength to fight one more battle or to take on another responsibility, consider how your actions will determine the outcome. Your job is to place your supporting cast and audience in a better situation. Knowing that you are responsible for the outcome provides a shot of energy from within that leads you to shine, despite your exhaustion and weariness.

I found educating and leading one of the hardest jobs I ever had. So to keep myself motivated I did little things to keep me from being overwhelmed. In my office I created a *wall of positivity*. Anytime I received an encouraging email from a parent or a teacher I posted it on the wall. Drawings from students, birthday cards, compliments from staff, poems and quotes were all posted as a source of reflection. In the moment of distress I would notify my secretary that I needed a minute to regroup. I would shut my office door and re-read what was posted on the wall of positivity. Remembering the moments when I received the positive feedback helped me to believe that all my efforts would eventually pay off. When the wall just wasn't enough, the students came to my rescue.

Students play a big part in providing encouragement and stress relief as well. I learned to value the different perspectives of my students. Often I would sit with students during a lunch period and talk about life. What was the latest gossip in reality TV? Sometimes I would even ask their opinion of my most recent music download. I'd ask the kids about movies, fashion, hairstyles, video games, social media trends, just about anything that would remind me in a moment of stress that there is more going on in this world than my job. In fact, social media was one of my most used coping tools as an educator. Social media ironically brought about an unexpected inspiration to my whirlwind of a career and an opportunity for me to encourage others, especially students and teachers. Most recently in my career I began to post motivational quotes on my Twitter and Instagram accounts that were relevant to what I was experiencing and hopefully beneficial to a fellow educator in suffering. Overtime, I found that former students would comment on the quotes and reply with testimonies of the experience they had as a student of mine. You see, being an advocate for students was a natural skill for me. Making a connection to people was the easiest part of my job as an educator. The feedback I was surprisingly receiving was encouraging to me and made me feel effective. It also pushed me to encourage and motivate even more people.

The term busy was an understatement in my most current role. My office was a revolving door that was used from the first bell in the morning until well after dismissal. I'd been told that being a leader who was approachable and available was highly respected so I became accustomed to completing tasks well after hours, in the evenings, and on the weekends. Most of the time it would be teachers and parents that utilized the seating in my office. Every now and then a student would drop by with the hopes of circumventing their counselor in regards to a schedule change or to complain about an instructor. Despite feeling like I was sitting in a vat of quicksand with all the deadlines and decisions that needed to be made, I made every effort to welcome, entertain, decision-make and solve problems. The highlight of it all was a senior student that made his way into my office to do the exact opposite of complain; he just wanted to listen.

One day I was working feverishly to meet a deadline that would potential effect maybe a couple thousand students or so, I was hoping not to be interrupted. As I stared at the computer monitor, out of the corner of my eye I saw a young man sashay his way in a take a seat as if he had a standing reservation.

"Hello. How's your day? What are you working on? Hair is cute today. Only 104 days left." All of this would come out of his mouth with the use of one single breath.

The Lesson Plan: An Educator's Inspiration

"Hey..., ugh..., Thanks..., everything...," was my response without looking up from the computer screen and keyboard.

Then I reminded myself, sometimes you have to make a point to stop what you are doing and listen to others. It wasn't often a student could sneak past my secretary and into my office. It had to be important and honestly, I was glad that this student was thoughtful enough to stop by. I stopped everything I was doing and turned to look at him.

As I looked at him, I thought about my senior year and a teacher I had that probably thought of me as the biggest pain in the butt, but I adored her. There were days when I know she would have much rather ate her lunch in peace than to answer my questions. I immediately thought to myself, "Could I be this person for this student?" He deserved the time that, I felt was non-existent. As we sat and talked, I forgot about my deadline. With him being engaged in our conversation and focused on my comments we both lost track of time. The conversation went from worrying about the current moment to contemplating what if. Somehow in the conversation, I explained to him my need to extend my reach as an educator and what I wanted to pursue. What couldn't have been more than 10 minutes, turned into a discussion about putting plans in place for the future and living out our dreams. As he ran out of my office, attempting to beat the tardy bell, I smiled, looked to the ceiling and whispered to myself, "Thank you."

His visit allowed me to take a quick break and put the day's challenges into perspective. The advice that I just gave to this student, I needed to tell myself for quite some time. Speaking with him left me with a burning fire to break out of my comfort zone and put my words into action. It wouldn't be until a few days later that the same young man would also fill my heart with a rush of joy and cause tears to drop on my desk cluttered with paperwork.

After walking out of a staff meeting and returning to my office, I was surprised to see an envelope placed on my seat. This small package didn't mimic the appearance of the usually dreaded manila envelopes that contained another task. I walked back to my door to close it, assuming I would need some time with this one. I sat, opened the envelope with a puzzled expression and began to read:

"Everyone may not understand your vision...But I do! Aspire to be great. Everyone and everything else will fall in place."

This by far was the most encouraging event to confirm that my efforts did in fact make an impact on a child's life. His act of kindness gave me hope for my own future and did in fact inspire me to keep believing in myself.

If you are not yet an educator but are working towards becoming one, I share this story with you in hopes that you too will one day motivate a student to pursue their dreams. The feeling is priceless and unforgettable. If you feel you have a natural knack of convincing others of their possibilities, teaching is the perfect arena for your skill.

The Lesson Plan: An Educator's Inspiration

If you are an educator, you may have experienced a student's encouraging words countless times. As educators, you know that the feeling of reassurance from your kids never gets old. The reward of teaching is paid at random times but always happens at the right moments. Remember these are the moments that you work for as a teacher, thus you are never under paid.

The Lesson Plan: An Educator's Inspiration
Determine What Motivates YOU
Only you know the reason why you make the decisions in your personal and professional life. Identifying your own way of coping is very important to your stability as a professional.

Continually Seek Intrinsic Rewards
Money is necessary to survive in this world, but it can never be your sole motivation. You must find value in having a sense of pride in your character and your level of influence on others. Leaving a legacy of

respect and commitment to others stays within the hearts and minds of the people you have reached. There is no monetary value that can be placed on such a feeling.

Have an Open Door and an Open Heart
The events that take place in a school day are unpredictable. There will be demands and you will be required to meet deadlines and remain on pace with curriculum standards. Unfortunately, your role as a caring leader will be most remembered by your staff, students, and parents well after the deadlines are met. The moments that you set aside for others could be unexpectedly returned when you find yourself in need of encouragement.

Motivating Others as a Means to Motivate Yourself
Over the years, I found that I got a surge of energy seeing the look on the faces of others when they were excited about doing something for themselves. The way I see it, being surrounding by a team of

confident and enthusiastic people only makes the goal that much more attainable. It also helps relieve individual pressure to reach the goal. Find opportunities to recognize and encourage the people around you. Building the character of others is a sign of your own character.

No matter where you are at in your professional journey, you have the ability to be a leader. Regardless, if you are a student, teacher, or if you are an experienced administrator, there is leadership needed on every level of life. Motivate yourself to take the lead.

The Lesson Plan

Chapter 13

An Educator Inspired

The Lesson Plan: An Educator's Inspiration

"I have always been told it's lonely at the top. So before I head in that direction I plan to bring someone with me." K.L. Herald

Two weeks of holiday vacation was relaxing yet, it allowed for self-reflection and goal setting. Playing the conversation over in my head and repeatedly reading the card that was left on my desk, there was obviously a flame burning within. Over the Christmas break the decision was made to take a risk and seriously consider taking a new direction in my life. Returning to work at the start of the new year marked the beginning of what I like to call, educating the educator.

No one around me understood where the sudden change in attitude and surge of motivation stemmed from. Naturally, I am self-motivated and driven. But now at the start of a new year, I knew the time had finally come. Here I was preaching to student's day in and day out to become whoever and whatever their heart desired. In actuality, I was living in fear of taking my own advice.

Being an educator came naturally and don't get me wrong, I love the interaction with teachers and students. However, deep inside I couldn't help to feel as if there was a challenge for me that I had to seek. The same opportunities that were in place to support others were also available to assist in accomplishing my own dreams and goals. The more I thought about it, the more I became angry at my own perception. I was speaking as a genius and acting like a fool. Frequently speaking to students, co-workers and even strangers about living a life without limitation, somehow I managed to cage my desires. And here I was trying to convince others to dream the ultimate dream, yet allowing my own dreams to remain concealed. Shaking my head in the mirror, I realized that my words were less convincing to students and more of a disappointment to myself. Immediately I viewed myself as an invalid resource.

Comparable to a salesman soliciting a service he would never purchase himself, I had yet to be convinced enough to buy my own product. A change was well overdue and the courage to explore motivating beyond the confines of a public school abruptly surfaced. Besides, as I replayed a recent incident that took place over Christmas break, I wanted even more to step out of my comfort zone and make a difference.

As I sat mingling with family and friends, I made a joke to a family member that wasn't received the way I intended. To be honest, the joke was more of me uttering a dream aloud. As people were complimenting me on the new house and how nice the kitchen was, they also made mention to the fact that I didn't know my way around a kitchen.

"What on earth are you going to do with a kitchen this size? A relative said in a humorous tone.

I laughed and jokingly said, "It's for the personal chef I will hire one day." With that comment, my relative not only laughed harder but turned away as if I had just made the most asinine comment. As my eyes welled, the taste of my own tears served as a dose of reality and a reminder it wasn't too late to make a change. As for my life, I would follow the direction of my heart and mind. It wasn't about having a personal chef to prepare meals. What hurt me the most was that the people I loved no longer had an imagination. Life somehow managed to strip them of the ability to dream and work towards making their dreams come true. As I leaned over the counter I looked down to hide the tears that were splashing onto the granite. Standing over my head I could hear my mother say in a sharp tone,

"Stop telling people your dreams. Stop talking and show them!"

I looked up to my mother through my swollen eyes and asked, "At what point do people stop dreaming? I just don't understand it. I know that I can make anything I want happen. I don't ever want to stop dreaming and planning out my life." My words sneaked out of my mouth like a 5 year old child.

As mom stood there preparing Christmas dinner in the kitchen of her dreams she looked at me with the most serious eyes I ever remembering seeing.

"Don't ever stop. I raised you to be and do whatever you can think of. Now do it. I will be here to encourage you every step of the way."

In that moment her words gave me the strength to move forward with my goals and the fuel to bring it all to fruition. In that moment I decided to take a silent leap of faith and made the prediction on who would be the last to laugh. Now at the age of 34, I would step out of my own comfort zone and embrace what I believed to be my natural God given gift. Somehow I would make people see their potential and move towards accomplishing their dreams.

The Lesson Plan: An Educator's Inspiration

This journey would no longer be about my personal aspirations to climb the career ladder. The rat race of being promoted and adjusting only to readjust and work towards being promoted again was tiring. What was I trying to prove? What I was portraying on the outside may have been what was necessary to be a school leader, but my heart and mind was being compressed. A career of rat racing would only lead to fatigue and loneliness. Ascending the ladder only to look down at others that needed your help, yet being too tasked to take an interest in others became the norm. The realization arose, a true test of my ability to lead and motivate would be to extend my commitment into the surrounding community, possibly the entire state and maybe even the nation. But first I would motivate my own family to dream again. The first step in convincing my family and others would be to show them that anything is possible.

In just a few short years as an educator, I was blessed with a vast amount of knowledge and experience that prepared me to not only run the professional race, but to win it. Why not share what I had conveniently placed in my professional toolkit with others?

The Lesson Plan: An Educator's Inspiration
Natural Helpers

Helping others pursue their dreams is what we do as educators. We naturally want to show someone the right way or teach them the methods that will lead them to success. Helping others in your personal life is just as rewarding as helping the students at your school site. Make yourself available to others when they ask questions. You may not have all the answers, but your experience is unique to someone else's.

Life-Long Learning
"It's only too late to do something if your time has completely expired. If you still have time, you still have an opportunity." - K.L. Herald

The Lesson Plan

Chapter 14

The Toolkit

The Lesson Plan: An Educator's Inspiration

If you have made the conscious decision to consider a career in education or to work with children then you probably want the responsibility and reward of impacting someone's life. Each of us has a character trait that is unique and personalized. In your current job setting you may have experienced similar situations like the ones described here. Whether it is your ability to make a connection with the most challenging student or cleverly convince a sub-par educator that seeking professional development is the key to professional growth, we all bring something to the table. Some of us have more talent to share than others. Some people build upon their talents and others suppress their gifts. Working in the field of education I have found that most teachers and educational leaders have unique talents that go undisclosed unless someone or something unexpectedly occurs, revealing the magic.

Stereotypically, educators can't be considered cool or fun, when in reality educators have so much more to teach beside the content in textbooks or procedures in a safety manual.

Nonetheless, educators possess a knowledge base that is continuous. As educators, we are forced to research current trends and strategies that are effective for today's student population. We are continually seeking strategies that are researched-based to assist us in changing the lives of the students in our midst. Teachers provide a recipe that includes a heap of knowledge, mixed with a splash of patience and a dash of love. If you reserve a special place in your heart for children, you have met the most important requirement for the profession. If you have ever taught or instructed an individual and felt rewarded by their receptive response, you have felt the act of impacting a human life.

I tell you my story to emphasize the fact that however you ended up being a teacher, coach, mentor, or any form of educator; be thankful. With or without your acknowledgement, your gift of being able to educate others is something you can embrace. If you are considering a position in education, believe that it's part of your plan. You may be an individual that has a gift for naturally being able to make connections with others. If this is the case, you could probably go as far as to consider yourself a good person that could provide direction to an impressionable mind.

To be a leader, by most definitions, it would require that you set yourself apart from others. In the profession of education, primarily in the school setting, you may display traits of a leader if you find yourself stepping outside of your classroom, spearheading initiatives, and viewing the administration as allies rather than dictators. The ability to motivate and encourage your fellow co-workers may be a sign that you have what it takes to be a school leader.

There will be times when bad things happen. When working in any capacity with the general public, things will not always go as planned. There will be contact with various personalities that will be both frustrating and tiring. You can preplan, plan and plan again but in all honesty, you have no control over the outcome or what others will actually do. The decisions that other teachers make, the actions of students, and the concerns of parents are all unpredictable. Blaming yourself when a bad situation arises will not eliminate the fact that it happened. The most driven academic professional with a natural talent to influence a group of students couldn't circumvent a student from cheating if that is the students' intention. You can only control what you do and hopefully that is giving this profession your best.

If reading this leaves you questioning if educating, mentoring, or leading is right for you, I would encourage you to visit a school, youth facility or afterschool program. I would suggest you get a feel of your talent to work with children prior to making the commitment to directly impact a child's life.

If you are in the field as an educator, know that the toughest times will teach you the most valuable lessons. Nothing should ever be taken personal and remember that every lesson will fit perfectly in your professional toolkit.

The Lesson Plan: An Educator's Inspiration

The Lesson Plan: Professional Toolkit Necessities

- Research the position
- Don't be afraid to share your story
- Empower others
- Make connections
- Recognize and compliment colleagues
- Shadow/Observe/Listen
- Network
- Know your audience
- Humility
- Balance
- Faith
- Self-Motivation

The Lesson Plan

Chapter 15

Transparency

This is my story; my story as an average young woman, with the audacity to connect to others and the humility to share personal moments of despair. Beginning with what some considered a regular career and later pursing the dream of being an author and motivational speaker, here I am. Choosing to break barriers among people despite cultural differences and societal beliefs was one of the best decisions made in my life. Over the past 8 years, the field of education has helped to shape me into someone powerful enough to impact another human life. I've stated before in this work and I will go on to repeat myself, I believe that our lives have a plan that is beyond our realm of comprehension. There is no way I could have predicted that humility and despair would lead me to where I am now. Plan or no plan, this is my story.

The Lesson Plan: An Educator's Inspiration

As I sat at my computer working on the presentation for my first speaking engagement, an overwhelming feeling of anxiousness prevented me from staying focused. I wondered how I would be received. Predicting if the audience would be entertained and touched emotionally by my personal stories, I started to second guess my new venture. Would my words be enough to convey a powerful and motivating message to my unknown audience? Planning and marketing for a seminar geared to motivate educators was a huge task to take on in less than 2 months; even more challenging for someone with no experience in motivational speaking.

As I stood in front of the small crowd that consisted of mostly family and friends, I appreciated that my toughest critics were right in front of me. I said a short prayer to God asking him to give me the words that were meant to be shared. Nervously, I entered the room and spoke on what I knew the most about; connecting and motivating others. My prayers were answered. With an idea and a little help from family and friends, I pulled off my first motivational speaking event. This would be the first step in the direction of pursuing my dreams.

Before the seminar, I vowed that once the event was over I would take time to relax and rest before putting the finishing touches on my first publication. The time spent preparing for the event; I'd borrowed from my son. I needed to wind down, but my mind was racing with thoughts of the next seminar and changes I wanted to make. Extremely tired, all I wanted to do was delve into the stack of participant survey cards sitting in from of me.

The Lesson Plan: An Educator's Inspiration

I began to dissect the feedback received on the participant survey cards. As I searched through the stack looking only for the portion of the questionnaire that asked, "What did you like the least about the presentation?" I was interrupted by an unexpected video call from a very familiar face. As I looked down at my phone there was Ms. Basketball streaming in for a call.

"Well hello!" I exclaimed with complete surprise.

"Hey Ms. Herald, I just called to see how you were doing." She stated as she adjusted the phone so that we both would be in view through the small cell phone screen.

"I'm doing ok. How is school and basketball going? You haven't let the cold weather get you down have you?"

Even though we hadn't spoken in a few months, I always welcomed a call or letter from a former student. My fear is if I don't respond when they are reaching out, I may be a disappointment to them when they are in need of encouragement. As we completed our usual check in about popular pictures on Instagram, hair and the status of school; her classes and my job, she began to ask questions that were based on the recent changes that she was noticing in my life.

"What was that logo you posted online? How did you set up your website? Did you start your own company?"

The conversation with her that occurred almost a year ago came flooding back to my memory. Sitting on that video call answering all of her questions, I gleamed with an excitement no words could express. The fact that she was receptive to my advice and the information I was sharing was proof that my impact on her was just as powerful as her impact on me.

"What made you decide to start speaking to others?" she inquired.

At that moment I could have taken a step back in time and explained to her how her words completely caused a major self-evaluation which motivated me to pursue a new purpose in my life. I never mentioned the conversation to her and the feelings that trailed behind. She never knew the impact that she left in my heart and mind that day. The truth is, that conversation that took place a year ago was no longer important.

"I just want to help others." I said in a sincere tone.

As I ended the call, I made a promise to pursue this new direction in my life and provide my experience to others whenever asked. No matter what happened from that moment on, I would not allow another second to pass without taking action in my own life.

Was it meant for me to have a run in with a former principal about grammatical inaccuracies? Did crossing paths with troubled students in need of encouragement broaden my skills and help me to later work with adults? Was it the intention all along for that conversation with Ms. Basketball to be embedded in my mind and heart and to ultimately lead me to follow my own dreams? Everything happens for a reason. One thing is for sure, through

The Lesson Plan: An Educator's Inspiration

all of the challenges I have survived and remained in the field of education. As I sat and formulated the words to describe the occurrences of my career, I have no doubt every situation, conflict, and conversation was meant to happen. Somehow I was given the strength to withstand each moment, the knowledge to grow and the humility to transform my struggles into a transparent tale of events. Amazingly, a career in education was the ultimate blessing for me.

ABOUT THE AUTHOR

K.L. Herald is a Florida native, experienced educator and spirited motivational speaker. Her roots in the Tampa Bay area have been pivotal to the success of her career over the past decade. Humble beginnings as a Coordinator for youth organizations, such as the YMCA and Tampa Police League, sparked her passion to create more depth for her future.

In 2002, K. L. Herald obtained an undergraduate degree in Interdisciplinary Social Science from the University of South Florida. Shortly, after completing her undergraduate degree she was hired as a middle school History teacher for the School District of Hillsborough County. While settling into her career, K.L. also completed her Masters of Arts in Educational Leadership from Nova Southeastern University. One year after receiving her M.A., she was appointed to Assistant Principal of Student Affairs for a local high school.

In her role as a Dropout Prevention Specialist and

The Lesson Plan: An Educator's Inspiration

Assistant Principal for Student Affairs and Curriculum, K.L. worked hand-in-hand with students, teachers and parents. She observed countless opportunities to advance student success that were consistently being overlooked. Across the nation a neglect to place emphasis on education is becoming a disturbing reality. Test scores have dominated teacher goals and superseded the outcry to develop student self-esteem. In her first years as an Administrator, she rapidly became familiar with techniques to motivate not only students, but teachers and educational leaders as well.

K.L. Herald has set the tone by launching a leadership organization that illustrates strategies, accomplishments, and provisions to support the field of education and introduce others to the many possibilities that surface through higher learning. K. Herald Developments L.L.C. and K.L. Herald, Inc. were created as a source for intrinsic motivation for education, professional and personal aspects of life.

www.ingramcontent.com/pod-product-compliance
Lightning Source LLC
Chambersburg PA
CBHW071702090426
42738CB00009B/1632